Pure Blind Faith

Lisa Willice Silva

Copyright © 2013 Lisa Willice Silva

All rights reserved.

ISBN: 978-0-9856886-0-8

DEDICATION

I'm honored to dedicate this book to my awesome husband, Daryl C. Silva, my beautiful daughter Soleil Love, and my handsome son Ocean Peace. I couldn't ask for a better family. You were truly my vision of God's ultimate gift. I am truly Grateful and Blessed to have you all in my life, Thank you. I also want to Thank my "second" family. You know who you are. Your endless support is always appreciated.

Table of Content

1	The Discovery	4
2	PBF 101	9
3	MJ, Another PBF	15
4	A working actress/extra	18
5	Mary Poppins	23
6	5 Stages to seeing GOD	31
7	Mary Poppins Returns	40
8	Serenity & Peace	47
9	Heaven on Earth	50
10	Ultimate PBF	57
11	Love@aol	63
12	THE ONE!!!	77
13	PBF at work	87
14	Time to give up	92
15	GOD'S path	114
16	The Miracle	131
	My Testimony	147
	Special thanks.Contact Information	149

CHAPTER ONE
"THE DISCOVERY"

"Because you have so little faith. I tell you the truth, if you have faith as small as a mustard seed, you can say to this mountain, 'Move from here to there' and it will move. Nothing will be impossible for you." Matthew 17:20 (NIV)

"If you have faith as small as a mustard seed, you can say to this mulberry tree, 'Be uprooted and planted in the sea,' and it will obey you. Luke 17:6 (NIV)

If you asked me, I'd say, my faith was never the size of a mustard seed, my faith is more like the size of an Avocado seed. For years I wasn't aware that the amazing things I was inviting into my life were due to "Blind Faith." I spent years being blind to my own Blind Faith until it was revealed to me by not only 1 though 2 people. I truly believe God gives everyone a gift, for years I didn't know what my gift was, it just came natural to me, then I discovered my gift.

A few months ago, at a small group for the one of the churches we attend, I was asked to fill out a spiritual profile form, one of the questions asked,

"What is your spiritual gift? What makes you different from others? What gift did God give you that few people have?

I was puzzled. I thought, nothing really. I can't sing, oh, well, maybe a lullaby or two, my dancing is normal, nothing extravagant by any means. I can trace or copy a character to look similar to the real image, like what a coloring book would do. I love art and crafts though never mastered any of it. I love writing though never published or sold anything. I love backpacking and traveling, though hey, who doesn't, well at least I think so. I love being a mom, which I was well trained for after being a nanny in Los Angeles for 20 years, no surprises, it just came easy and natural. I love being a wife as well though I wouldn't call being married and loving your husband a gift, I'd call it love, I'd even call some of it fate.

I always tried to be the best sister to my sister, I always thought, "I want to be the big sister I wish I had." I wanted to be the best friend to my few chosen friends, the best sister to my three brothers, the best nanny, the best sister in law, the best daughter in law, the best wife to my husband and of course, the best mother to my children though that's not a gift, that's a choice. I thought then, "Wow, this is really hard. I don't think God gave me a gift?" How did I miss out on a special spiritual gift?

That day I was talking to my oldest brother Derek. I asked Derek, who's gifts are obvious, he's a talented artist, idealist, singer, songwriter and producer. I expressed to Derek, "You're so gifted, God gave you some awesome gifts that everyone knows about and sees. "God did not give me a gift, I don't have one." Derek said, "Lisa, are you kidding me? You don't know what your spiritual gift is?" I was shocked that he thought I had one. "No," I said with confidence. He says "Lisa I never met anyone who has as much Blind Faith as you do." I thought "Blind faith, that's a gift?!!" "Of course," he said. "Who believes as strongly as you do and actually lives on blind faith?"

After talking with Derek, I called my husband Daryl, who I call "Babe." His gifts are also very obvious, He's an Excellent Filmmaker, Writer, Director, he's a doer, not a talker, a great, loyal, all around person and now a man of God. "Babe", I said, "What is my spiritual gift?" He paused for a moment then said "Faith… Blind Faith" I thought "WOW… again I'm hearing that…unbelievable! "That's what Derek said." I said in shock.

A couple days later I'm sitting in my J way (Jesus's Way) Group, the word FAITH came up, I decided to talk about some of the things I've done based on Pure Faith. The girls were amazed at the crazy things I did in Blind Faith. Some people would call it gutsy, I've been told I'm a dreamer, I don't live in the real world, that I live in a fantasy world. That I manifest things because, or as my father would say, "Its already done," and I'm crazy enough to truly believe that it is indeed already done. A few of the girls in the group confessed they didn't have faith and could never just live based on Pure Faith alone. One confessed she has faith when it comes to others, however not for herself. I couldn't understand why they didn't believe it could happen for them? In this room of 12 or so girls, it appeared that no one had "Blind" Faith. That's when it hit me, I do have a gift that few have, and it really is Blind Faith.

Then one of the girls asked if I could pray for them to have that crazy kind of Faith. That blew my mind though I prayed and expressed that you have to believe in it, I, of course, can't be the only one believing in it for you. After days of pondering it in my head and talking to more people and telling of the different situations of Faith and them being amazed by it, I realized and understood that it was indeed a gift. After time, God laid it on my heart to write this book, as clear as you hear the voice of a family member or a friend, that's how clear the voice of God was to me when he suggested I do this. He put it in my head, I couldn't sleep that night and woke up writing everyday, all day for 7 days straight. The same amount of time God took to create the Earth, how ironic. Everything just flowed, the journey, the title, along with the cover. Seeing it's my spiritual gift, it made sense to share it with everyone who chooses to read it. Though the journey isn't over yet, this is the journey so far. With that in mind, this is, my story of Pure Blind Faith…

CHAPTER TWO
"PBF 101"

Looking back, I recall the first time I had PBF (Pure Blind Faith). When I was 11 years old I saw a commercial on TV with kids my age, walking on the beach on a sunny day, smiling, laughing, enjoying life. It was then apparent this was a commercial promoting travel to California, I was fascinated. It was so different from my hometown of Buffalo, New York where I was living at the time. I came to find out shortly afterwards that Los Angeles was part of California. I also learned that's where most celebrities lived, Michael Jackson and everyone who was in my teen magazine (Right On) lived, obviously because it was so beautiful. Sunshine almost every day, no snow, no blizzards, not very cold, one season, Summer, my favorite.

I then told my parents "I'm moving to Los Angeles when I turn 18." My father said "Who do you know in Los Angeles? "No one," I said, "though one day I will live there and my kids will be born there… California kids, like the kids on TV." I had a little cousin that lived in California who came to Buffalo who had never seen snow, I found that amazing.

Everyone ignored my desire, being only 11 years old at the time, it seemed like a far away dream to them. I spoke about it a lot over the years. When I turned 15, I bought maps and books on Los Angeles. I studied the maps, I knew that city, studied it North, South, East and West. I knew the streets, the different cities, how to get around, and where my favorite singer Michael Jackson lived...Encino!!!. "I will meet him one day," I said.

Growing up, based on the religious views of my parents, I wasn't allowed to go to the movies. My parents felt it supported the adult industry so we couldn't go. Now 17 years old, I snuck away to the movies with my High School friend Laurie. You would have thought I was on the Planet Mars. It was fascinating, I saw "The Incredible Shrinking Woman" with Lily Tomlin. If it was up to me, it would have won five Oscars. I was fascinated by the movie theatre, popcorn, seats and movie industry as a whole. My second sneak away movie was "Blue Lagoon" with Brooke Shields. The ocean was beautiful, the story was intriguing and the lifestyle was unimaginable. I was in awe of the movie.

To my dismay, my father found out I went to the movies, how, I don't know. He asked "What movie did you see?" Like always (trying to be the best daughter) I told the truth, "Blue Lagoon" and said proudly. "I heard about that movie," he said, "two naked people swimming around in the ocean!" I said, "No, it was a beautiful love story filmed on a beach, on a beautiful island." Needless to say, he didn't buy my admiration for it though it was worth the spanking and punishment that came with it. My brother Derek said I should have lied and said "Superman," which was also playing at the time. However in my mind, how could anyone not see the beauty in "The Blue Lagoon?" I guess neither of them appreciated it the way I did.

After that, unbeknownst to me, my PBF started. "I'm going to be an actress in Los Angeles, live near the ocean and do movies," I said. "I will live on a island," then it dawned on me, little did I realize I was already living on an island... Grand Island, NY near Niagara Falls. You could only enter it by bridge or boat. "Oh", I thought, I live on an Island. It didn't look like Blue Lagoon's Turtle Island though it was indeed an island. My mind was focused, my Faith was strong though it was time for college. "OK" I thought, "I'm studying theatre," so I'm ready when I move to LA.

My parents didn't approve of acting saying "it promotes lying." Your not who you say you are,"

11

they would say. Being that my father was religious and may understand from a religious perspective, I tried to point out to him that his favorite movie, "The Ten Commandments" with Charlton Heston as "Moses" was Charlton playing someone that wasn't him though look at how powerful that was, well, that didn't work. So I went to Daemen College in Buffalo, majored in Elementary/Special Education (for my parents) minored in theatre (for me) which didn't stand out and was overlooked. In my mind, Theatre was my major, that's all I really cared about.

Now 18 years old and in college, I went to NYC with Derek to see my college boyfriend who recently moved there, when I arrived on that particular trip, he surprised me with a marriage proposal. I wasn't ready for that at the time and my dreams, goals and focus was clearly 3,000 miles away. I respectfully declined his offer. I had faith that Los Angeles was in my future which I expressed to him. Marriage was not in my plans for now. He was a good guy though it was simply bad timing.

Back in college in Buffalo, now approaching 19 years old, I was sitting in a theatre class and the professor was talking about auditioning. He spoke about movies in LA, plays in NYC and how tough it will be when you get out there, rejection, rejection,

rejection. I thought, "Why am I sitting in class wasting time?"

I should be out in LA starting the tough road, the rejections that the professor is talking about. Its time to go to LA. I had no money, was a full-time student working in my father's supermarket, FIGMOS PTL (Finally I've Got My Own Supermarket, Praise the Lord) for free as many kids do working for their parents. How will I get money to go?

I had no doubt or fear of making that move, I just wanted to make it happen soon. Derek and my cousin Ricky had already moved to Florida. It was time for me to move but leaving my younger brothers, Jeff, Jason and especially my sister Jennifer was the hardest decision.

In my mind I was already in LA though clearly my body wasn't. Out of the blue one day, my cousin Iva called me and said " I'm going to Los Angeles for the summer, would you like to go with me?" "Oh my goodness, I've been planning to move there," I told her. She was surprised. Why she called me with this offer, I didn't know. However, I was very grateful. She was the niece of Musical Legend Rick James and her Aunt Penny (also Rick James's sister, my cousin) said we could stay with her at Teena

Marie's house, another Musical Legend for the summer. They said I could come and stay also.

Remember I studied my maps of Los Angeles, so I asked "Where does Teena live in LA? "Sherman Oaks!!!!" she said. "Oh my goodness, the city next to Encino, where Michael Jackson lived." This was my prayer being answered and to go there with a place to stay was definitely a bonus. I got up $300 and bought a $100 one way ticket to LA. I knew it would be the battle of my life to leave Buffalo, and it was. However it was my goal, my dream and my fate that gave me the strength to run away and go for it. Not to mention at 19 years old its not running away, however that's how it felt to me. I prayed all the way there, 5 hours of prayer that God would Bless my decision, my journey and my future. This was my first big experience with PBF. Little did I know that decision, that PBF, would change my families life and the next generations life. Everyone would eventually follow my journey to Los Angeles.

CHAPTER THREE
MJ, ANOTHER PBF

Palm trees, beaches, the Pacific Ocean, wow, another perfect day. LA was everything I imagined it would be and more. The bonus was that Michael Jackson lived a 1/2 mile away. I met Janet Jackson on her walk to the store, Latoya Jackson on a date outside the house though still hadn't met Michael, one of my PBF goals. After 3 months of living the Hollywood celebrity life with Teena, Penny and Rick James occasionally, Iva returned home to Buffalo, I didn't want to go back though I promised I would leave the day Iva left. So I went to Emeryville, Ca near San Francisco, to visit my cousin while Teena's secretary looked for an apartment for herself, the designer and myself. I stayed with my cousin for three weeks. We really bonded, she was a lot older than I was. She was more like an aunt than she was my cousin. I really enjoyed her, little did I know how important of a part I would play in her life years later.

Weeks after my visit to Emeryville, CA, I get the call that the girls got a roommate situation for me, to come back to claim my room in the apartment. I was sad to leave my cousin though happy to be back in LA and start my permanent life. I didn't embrace church however I had a personal relationship with God and had faith HE would always be there for me. I was very grateful for my new LA dream life.

I started my acting life by doing extra work on movie sets. Then the big day came, I was cast as a extra in the Pepsi commercial starring none other than Yes, Michael Jackson. I had only been in LA for a year or 2 now so accomplishing another PBF goal was of course very exciting.

Excitingly, I went to the 2 day commercial shoot, they picked me out of 200 girls to go back stage for a rehearsal, to scream when Michael ran by.

I walked backstage and Michael was just standing there, like it was no big deal, waiting for his cue to walk on stage and rehearse. He looked at me and smiled. I smiled back and he told me I looked like a teenage singer he was on tour with, then he sneezed on me. He sincerely apologized though God must have done that on purpose cause from that day on I realized he was human just like me. It was as clear as crystal that the message was "not to idolize anyone."

From that day on, I never idolized anyone again. I took down his posters that night and just looked at him as a great singer/performer, no longer as a "Teen Idol". The next day was the shoot and I was going into the audience, they were assigning seats. I said to myself, if I had to sit in a seat somewhere it was going to be front and center...PBF...as I was praying that prayer, one of the casting people pointed at me and said I want this young lady to sit right here.........in the first row, center seat, directly in front of the stage.

"Wow, did he read my mind or hear my prayer? Is God directing this shoot?" I thought. Well, as history showed, this was not only a life changing path for me though for Michael as well. He caught on fire during the first take which was the beginning of his new dangerous path. I was so close I could have grabbed him, though someone else grabbed him first. I just remember looking at him and thinking,"Why is his head glowing? I didn't remember that happening in rehearsal. That was pretty traumatizing, my prayers were with him. Though no more thoughts of meeting Michael, I moved on to my life in LA as an actress, well, an extra.

CHAPTER FOUR
A WORKING ACTRESS/EXTRA

No more celebrity life with rock stars, freebies, no more dreams of meeting MJ, no fancy cars or limos. I was on my own, on the buses of LA, learning the city and living my dream career.

Once I went on an audition which was in the San Fernando Valley of LA about an hour bus ride to the address I was given from where I lived. I got off the bus and walked to the address. As I approached the address it was someone's house, which surprised me. I expected an office building or studio.

I felt uncomfortable being at the front door of that house, looking at the address, hoping I was at the wrong address. God spoke to me and told me to go home. Amazingly, it felt as if my feet were disabling me from walking the 8 stairs it took to get to the doorbell. At that time, I didn't think of it as God talking to me, I was just overwhelmed with a really bad feeling, instincts.

After the hour bus ride there, I was fighting my instinct to just ring the doorbell though I couldn't get myself to walk up the stairs and ring it. So I turned around, walked back to the bus stop and went home. I never knew and will never know what was behind that door. However God obviously did and told me to go home, I'm eternally grateful for that. No more auditions from unknown individuals in odd locations. Little did I realize years later, based on bad experiences, this would clearly become a suggestion for all actors/actresses in every acting publication that was out there.

I then, went and joined every casting agency for extras in LA. I was working and living off of extra work, learning the business from just about every set in town. I was a working actress, well, again, an extra. Cagney and Lacey was a big detective show at that time. I was so excited to work on that set. I didn't have a car though as I learned the city of LA with a map, I also learned the bus route with a map as well.

After a full day of working on the set of Cagney and Lacey, I knew the last bus came at midnight. The set was at a warehouse (stage) in the middle of nowhere. The Director said "Its a wrap," it was 11:58pm. I grabbed my things and ran to the bus stop across the street. Everyone was jumping in their car and leaving. The bus stop was across the street from the stage with a bus sign and a bench in an empty gravel filled lot.

Pure Blind Faith

As I stood there, everyone was gone from across the street. Just a quiet midnight wind and me standing at that bus stop in the middle of nowhere. 12:15am, 12:25am, I stood there thinking, "my goodness, I missed the last bus, what am I going to do?" As I was talking to God and myself, a truck drove by with 4 guys in it. They looked at me as they drove by, the car then stopped, they looked back and started to make a U Turn on this dead quiet deserted road that only I stood on.

I was scared to death, it was after midnight. They passed by me on the other side of the street pointing at me as they went by looking mean. I walked behind the bench in fear of them. I started praying, "Lord please get me out of this situation, please Lord make me disappear in these guys eyes, please Lord please." I'm crying and staring at the truck, both at the same time. I see the guys in the truck make another U Turn towards me, on my side of the street. "Help me Lord," I said as I watched these guys head towards me with a nasty smirk on their face. A bus then appeared in front of the truck and stopped to pick me up. "Thank you, Thank you, Thank you Lord," I said. I never saw that bus coming. I don't know where it came from. Though it was in front of the truck and I was able to get on. The

Pure Blind Faith

truck then went around the bus and left, "Amen," I thought. However, the night wasn't over.

I had to transfer to another bus that took me home. Now 1:00am, I had to get off at another bus stop. This one was in front of a railroad track with a bus stop sign and a liquor store across the street. A drunk was in front of the liquor store, he looked at me, standing there alone. "Oh Lord, here I go again," I thought. At least he's drunk, "Maybe I could fight him off?" He started to walk across the street toward me. I was scared though ready to fight. He's walking across the street talking to me in his drunken voice and holding his paper bag, shaped like a bottle. All of sudden, he turned around and walked back toward the liquor store, in the middle of the street. This shocked me, I felt someone standing behind me. I then looked back and a man was standing there looking like Abraham Lincoln, yes, Abraham Lincoln!!! I don't remember his face though my first thought was Abe Lincoln. He had on an old suit, something that Abe Lincoln would wear.

There's nothing there but railroad tracks and an empty field. A bus didn't drive by to drop him off, so where did he come from? He looked at me and smiled. I looked at him smiled and nodded my head to thank him for scaring the drunk guy away. He just smiled a mild smile back and a nod to the head as to say "Your welcome". The Abe Lincoln looking guy just made all my fears go away. Normally, I would have feared him. I mean after all he was a stranger. However he was different, it felt different, I felt relieved. The bus came about 10 minutes later, Abe stood there and didn't speak or move. I couldn't help it though I found myself looking back at him often. I got on the bus, then Abe got on and I watched him sit down. I then looked forward to make sure I didn't miss the stop closest to my apartment. As I got closer to my stop, I looked back to thank Abe again, his seat was empty. The bus hadn't stopped at all, I asked the bus driver, "What happened to the guy that looked like Abe Lincoln? The bus driver said "What guy?" I then said "The guy that got on the bus with me?" He said "I didn't see no guy, you got on the bus alone." Keep in mind I wasn't on, neither have I taken any drugs or did I drink, I was as shocked and surprised as you all are right now. Umm……..I think God wanted to build my Faith. He desired me to have a greater trust in him and let me know HE'S always there with me.

CHAPTER FIVE
"MARY POPPINS"

Well, needless to say, I had done and was continuing to do a lot of extra work, I got small roles in a few movies. I did a TV drama series. I was seen in a few times in the Cosby sitcom "A Different World," starring Lisa Bonet & Jada Pinkett, now Jada Pinkett Smith of course. I was in many music videos, one with Morris Day, lead singer of the famous 80's group, The Time. The song was "Oak Tree" and was an amazing experience. I also did countless numbers of other things that I can't remember, my extra resume was endless at the time.

One day I was so upset because I lost $90 which seemed like $900. I needed to pay my phone bill. I was crying and asking God to help me find it or at least earn another $90 before they disconnected my phone. A couple days later I went to get into my car, as I was opening the car door a $50 bill was rolled up on the ground beside the car. I could see the number 50 on the bill, I was so excited. As I unrolled it, there was a $50, $20, and another $20 bill. I was praying and thanking God. I knew it wasn't the money I had lost because I had all 20's and a $10. Another prayer answered, Thank you Lord.

Shortly after finding this money, I auditioned for a big casting director, I was so nervous I didn't do a good job. I totally bombed and come to find out it was for "Jo Jo Dancer", the life story of Legendary Comedian Richard Pryor, I auditioned to play one of his wives. After that day, I promised myself to never let anyone intimate me or make me feel that nervous. The only one I will fear is God himself. To this day, I live by that.

After my brother Derek moved to LA a year later, I now had a few years of extra work, bus riding and struggling under my belt. I felt I could do more, make more money, buy a car, have a break on rent/bills and still learn the industry. Derek had a girlfriend and they seemed to be okay. I prayed for the perfect job.

My prayer was, "I wanna be able to learn the industry, make stable money, have a live-in job somewhere and have a car." I looked into some nanny agencies and landed my first job, working for an A-list Actor. I had access to the family's car, made good money, learned the industry and lived-in with a $100 grocery bonus and over looking all of Los Angeles through their garage apartment.

However in my prayers, I forgot to ask for a good kid. This kid would curse at you, F... you was a typical morning greeting from him, they believed in letting him express himself. Well, needless to say he was doing just that. After a short time, I simply couldn't take it anymore. I expressed myself and quit. I then became an nanny for a entertainment CPA for 2 years. I prayed for the same goals, to be a live-in, have access to a car, good money and I remembered to pray for nice kids. However I now forgot to pray for a loving family. Shortly after getting this new job now, I found out the father was cheating on the mother with her best friend. Being a person who believes in honor, I stayed until I couldn't take it anymore and moved on.

Now a nanny with 3 years of experience, I refocused and said "Lord, I'm ready to travel." So I prayed for a family that travels, loves each other, for my own car and a lot more money. Little did I know how strong my prayers were, how strong my faith was, I was again truly blind to my own Blind Faith. I knew God would grant me exactly what I prayed for and boy did he do just that. I turned down a lot of jobs until I clearly heard the answer to what I prayed for.

Pure Blind Faith

I was offered a job with a metaphysical channeller. I didn't know exactly what she did though I was hired on the spot. They told me I didn't have to believe in what she was doing. Her beliefs were not a part of my nanny duties for her 2 1/2 year old son. I would start the following day, make good money and my first day of work would be in Hawaii. Wow, did God answer my prayers or what!!! I came home to tell my family what had happened in the interview and that I was leaving for Hawaii the next day. After leaving and not hearing from me for a few days, Derek went crazy, he thought I ran to Hawaii with a cult. I finally called and assured him I was fine.

It was the most stressful job I had to date, so let's break down my faith based prayer. First of all, I prayed for a car of my own. When we got back from Hawaii, I told my employer I didn't have a car. She instantly gave me the staff's car, a Toyota Corolla for the price of a penny, literally, we exchanged a penny. Funny enough I would learn years later that my future mother in law would enjoy this same exchange with her father in exchange for her home, love these coincidences. Needless to say, my boss giving me the car made me unpopular with the staff, especially when she announced they could no longer drive the car, its Lisa's car now. "My nanny needs a car," she said. If my nannies happy, my kid is happy," she said. Well, it made sense to me. I appreciated it and was happy to finally have a car. However, I of course, didn't want to start off on the staff's bad side though all was okay with them, in time.

Secondly I prayed for more money and to travel, not only did I make good money though my boss gave me $300 a day for her 2 1/2 year old son's daily activities as she did her metaphysical seminars. By the end of the week I would have $1,000 leftover and would give it back to her with receipts. She would say "Lisa, I gave you that money to do things with my son, if you're giving it back to me you haven't done enough and I don't need the receipt." Then she would hand me another envelope with another $300. I was so stressed out over this money. I couldn't bank it, as people advised me too. That would have been dishonest and stealing. "If I didn't spend it, I wasn't doing enough for her son," I just kept hearing that in my head.

The pressure was on, I would take him to the museum, the zoo and amusement parks anywhere USA, wherever we were. She asked me to stay within a hour's drive or plane ride to her in case of an emergency and always come home at night. I loved when we went to Florida cause I could get on a plane and go to an amusement park within an hours time and the money would be spent doing everything First Class. I would go to the gift shop and buy the biggest life-sized stuff animal I could find. I bought a life sized giraffe at $700 and an elephant at $800. Though the 3 year old was getting bored with life. He did so much, he was unmoved by every event. And yes, I got rid of the money every week, amen, sometimes giving it to the homeless.

    I started hating these envelopes I'd receive everyday for $300. I couldn't wait to have a day off and not feel pressured to spend a dime. My personal money just built up in my account. Now living in LA, I would hand my brother Jeff my ATM card and leave for weeks. He would spend all the money in it and I didn't care. It would fill up again in two weeks with my pay that I wouldn't touch or spend. I now hated money, shopping or even seeing it. This went on for 2 years, extreme traveling with extreme amounts of daily money.
    I was going crazy, crying and stressing out. I know it sounds crazy, trust me though if you've ever seen the movie "Brewster's Millions" starring Richard Pryor, you'll understand my 2 year struggle. Oh, did I pray for a loving family? I liked my boss though she was loving both men and women, so it's safe to say there was definitely a lot of loving going on. I never knew who was in her bed and told her

this of course wasn't healthy for her son to see every morning. She agreed as well, my big mouth now got me a roommate, she moved her son into my room.

No one truly understood what I was going through, my mom (now divorced) and siblings, encouraged me to stay at that job. "You're making a lot of money, why would you leave, just spend the money," they would say. Of course Jeff didn't want me to leave, he was spending my personal money. I didn't care, I didn't want to hear the word money again. I was hating money. Needless to say, after 2 years, I quit!!! I felt from that day on, God taught me that even though money is essential in our survival, it would not be my god nor would material things. I live by that motto to this day

With absolutely no money in my account, I was broke and didn't care at first, though now I couldn't pay rent, my phone bill or anything. I took a long break, sold the car my boss had given me and bought a ticket to Buffalo. After being in Buffalo for six months, I was ready to go back to LA. I had no money or anything to get my life back in LA. I prayed and said "Lord, I want to go back to LA, please send me back." I started packing and getting ready for my return not knowing how I would get back there.

Then I get a phone call, it was one of my older cousins, I was asked if I was available to go to Emeryville, CA and take care of my cousin who I had visited a few years prior, bonded with and kept in touch with over the years. Her brother told me she was now dying of cancer and the family would buy my ticket to California. He asked that I stay a month until he could come. I was happy to go back to the West Coast and was honored to be there for her as she was there for me many years back.

CHAPTER SIX
5 STAGES TO SEEING GOD

When I arrived in Emeryville, after years of talking to my cousin though not seeing her, I walked into her house to find her bedridden. She looked at me then this big grin came over her face. I was thanking God for the bonding we had built many years ago, because prior to that we didn't really know each other. We had never had a conversation just "Hi" and "Bye" like you often have with your older relatives.

She said "Lisa look what they did to me!" She then lifted her shirt up and there was nothing there, I mean nothing, no breasts, just a stitch line in the middle of what once were breasts. This of course took me back, I tried not to react. She handed me this soft gooey sack, I had no clue what it was. She said "that's my breast Lisa, that's my breast!" I excused myself and went into the bathroom and cried. She started calling me, "Lisa" she hollered, "Are you okay?" I said, "I'm okay, "I'll be out in a minute." "Lisa, don't let this happen to you," she said. I told her "I don't know what to do to prevent this."

My grandmother had come for a few weeks to help her though grandma said my cousin had been very mean to her. She felt grandma was older and couldn't understand why this happened to her, being much younger at 55 when grandma was well into her 70's. Grandma left, she couldn't take it. I guess thats why they called me. Everyone knew that my cousin and I had bonded years ago and she spoke highly of me over the years, as I did of her.

As days went by, my cousin and I bonded even closer. She went through all the stages of death which I later learned about. I wondered where all her friends were. She had very close friends that I met years ago. When I asked her, she told me why she ended each relationship. Each explanation was elementary. Finally she admitted to me later, she didn't want them to see her dying so she ended the relationships.

Stage 1- Denial & Isolation

I began to drive her to her Chemo treatments, the first time I went they put me in a room and I waited for her. All of a sudden, I heard screaming, I asked the nurse if that was my cousin screaming. She said "Please come in, she's going crazy thinking your getting radiation poisoning." "Me?" I said. "Why would she think I was getting radiation poisoning?" I said. I ran into the room. She asked me if I was okay "They're poisoning you!" She screamed. I assured her I was fine and will continue to wait for her outside if she's continues to worried. The nurse then agreed to get me when she was done. She calmed down. That became our routine from that day on. She goes to Chemo, I wait outside the building.

I took her to see her doctor after about a week. She looked at her doctor and asked for another pill or treatment. The doctor said "Listen, no more pills, no more treatments, its time to go." "Nothing else? She asked. "Nothing!!!" he said, "our journey is complete." My heart dropped. She asked "How long do I have?" The doctor said sadly, "A few weeks." That was the quietest ride home I ever had, we were both teary eyed and silent.

As time went on, she became weaker and weaker. She was very tall and I, being short, of course made it very hard for me to help her to the bathroom or pick her up when she fell. I wasn't a nurse or had any training as one. I called her siblings in Buffalo, they were great about helping me get through this. They felt it was time to put her in a nursing home.

STAGE 2- Anger Stage

The siblings arranged the nursing home stay so I took her. When she got settled in, she was quick to get into bed and relax. I laid with her hugging her silently. We exchanged no words for about an hour. I then told her I will come everyday for lunch and dinner. I got the schedule and made it my daily routine. I had breakfast at the house, then lunch with her, went back to the house then back to have dinner with her, every day I did this. She had them bring me lunch and dinner also. So in our minds it was a fine restaurant. After a few days, I put her in a wheelchair and took her for a walk.

It was an exceptionally bright and beautiful day. Little did I know, it would bring her so much anger. Everyone we'd walk by, she'd say, "Why does she get to live? Why does he get to live? "Look at her smiling, she gets to live," she expressed in anger.

Her brother was a Pastor. He would try and talk to her about God, though she was hating God and hating her brother's calls. He was a big help to me through it all as she and I had never talked about God.

She and I had the most beautiful lunches and dinners.Laughing and talking, for a moment we forgot about where we were, and why we were there. I told my stories about LA, acting and nanny life, she would tell her stories about her life and friends. We were just old pals hanging out. It was fun for both of us.

Feeling like an old pal, I thought of her old friends and how close they were. When I got home that night, I decided to go through her phone book and call them. I knew she didn't want them to see her in that condition, I respected that, though I felt that they should not leave on such bad terms. So I kind of repaired the damage she did. Many of them thanked me for calling and I cried with a few of them. They understood her pride.

STAGE 3- Bargaining Stage

During lunch, she said, "I was wondering if I did more charity or more good deeds, would God let me live longer? Maybe I shouldn't have smoked." she said. Well, I thought, I want to change her thoughts around. It was such a beautiful sunny day, why should she miss it cause she was hating everyone walking, talking and living. So I said, "Hey, why don't we start by going outside, walking around and wondering how long people have to live? I then wheeled her outside and asked her as I was pointing to a lady walking by, "How long do you think God will give her? What do you think she will die of?" I would say. She would answer it and we came to the conclusion that we would all die one day, when our time comes.

Stage 4- Depression Stage

This lasted for a few days, I was able to take her out each day though she was beginning to be very quiet. Our conversations slowly depleted. I just pushed her around and didn't speak unless she spoke. I had never experienced this before so I just let her lead and was happy she was enjoying the sunshine, thinking, thinking and thinking. One day during our walk she looked at me and said, "Lisa you have to go on with your life." "You can't stay here forever." I assured her my time was spent with her right now and I had nothing else to do but to be with her.

She was getting weaker and no longer ate her lunch or dinner. I was feeding her very little of it. Our lunches were very quiet. At dinners she was very weak and ate nothing at all. I knew I was losing my pal, she knew as well. Her brother was coming to take over and I was leaving the next day. I had been there a month, I knew it was a matter of days. I packed the house as the family asked me to do. Then I went to see her on the last day, only this time it was for breakfast. Her brother was on his way to take over and I was on my way to the bus station heading back to LA to start my life over again. I knew she didn't want to see her brother, the Pastor, knowing he would preach to her.

Stage 5- Acceptance Stage

We knew it was our last day together and this time it was different. She saved all her energy for this last meal together. She rarely ate her breakfast, we talked about death, we laughed about death. I asked her to help me win the lottery on the other side, we laughed and made a pact for her to come back and visit me one day in LA. She said if she can, she will visit me. "Make sure I know it's you," I said. "Oh you'll know its me," she laughed. Then things got very quiet, she looked at me and said, "Lisa you've been in church all your life, right?" "Yes" I said. "I don't go to church in LA however." "You know a lot about God?" she said. "I think I do." I innocently said. "Lisa," she said "how do I get into Heaven?" My heart sunk. I felt that her path to heaven or hell was in my hands. If I didn't tell her the right thing and she went to hell it would be my fault. I felt so overwhelmed. Her fate fell on my shoulders. I said, "I was forced to go to church all my life." "I didn't listen when I was there." She said "Though you know, you know how to get me to heaven." I said, "All I know is that if you ask God to forgive you for your sins and if you mean it in your heart, he will forgive you."

Next thing I knew she started confessing her sins to me. "Whoa!!!" I said to her, "this is between you and God." I knew it was time to go, we embraced and held each other. I said "Have fun in Heaven." I walked out the door and looked back. I saw her talking and confessing. She looked at me with the most beautiful smile on her face, it was Heavenly. Tears fell down her face and mine. We exchanged smiles, bright smiles. I then headed to the bus station to go back to LA.

As I arrived back in LA, her brother called me. He was crying, barely able to speak, he said, "Lisa, she's gone." He didn't get to talk to her. She died before he got there. He was crying saying he wasn't able to get her to Heaven, she cursed God and hated him," he said. I then told him about our last conversation. He asked me "What did you say to her?" I then told him about our spiritual encounter. He stopped crying and said "Lisa, you did well" He was so relieved. It's like you could see his smile thru the phone. I was so relieved as well, wow, what a burden lifted. Thank you Lord for giving me that wisdom and knowledge when I needed it. I was and continue to be eternally grateful.

CHAPTER SEVEN
MARY POPPINS RETURNS

When I got back to LA, I thought about my cousin Joyce a lot. I would laugh and cry though in time all things healed and life was beginning again. I had now been in LA for a few years, I knew it well. I got back to my life and was now saying a new prayer. "Lord, I don't want to travel anymore, just stay in LA and work more of a 9-5 nanny job with a 9-5 normal family, that I could bond with and really love. No more living-in though with just enough money to pay my bills." I went on quite a few interviews with actors, actresses, singers, producers, even a very famous talk show sidekick, all well known, very famous though I was so over the Hollywood garbage. I wasn't interested in any of these jobs. My agency was telling me that it'd be difficult to find what I was looking for. Hollywood people are not 9-5, they travel a lot, homes everywhere. She said she didn't have anything else for me.

I was willing to wait it out. Its out there, I know it is. One family was calling and really wanted to hire me, she tried to get me to take it temporarily. I had no money, no car and no job. Though I knew God would bring the right family to me. I told her I was waiting on God's Blessing. I didn't want to get attached to another child and leave. I wanted a child or children I could watch grow up. I didn't want to be a temporary nanny, I wanted to be a permanent one.

A few weeks later, my agency called, she was excited. "A family came in that I think you're great for," she said. The parents are divorced and the kids go back and forth. The parents live around the corner from each other and they get along really well. There's no fighting or bitterness. He's a Director with a set schedule, he does TV shows and has a 9-5 schedule. They have 2 kids, ages 5 and 7 and most of all, they don't travel. Maybe a family trip here and there though nothing crazy and its a live-out situation. They're willing to let you drive their car until you get one. They've been interviewing a lot of people and they can't find what they're looking for. I really want you to go on this interview," she said. Needless to say, I was excited to go.

I went on the interview to meet the mother and kids. The little girl was 5 years old. She was sitting on the couch with this bright little smile on her face and asked me a few questions. The mom was very nice, fit and naturally pretty, not the typical Hollywood fake pretty. She was giggly, happy and bouncy, I liked her, she was real. The 7 years old son was quiet though you could tell he was clever and was listening closely. Then I drove around the corner to meet their dad, I loved him. He was so cool. Not the typical Hollywood outrageous Director. He was normal, at least normal enough. I liked them a lot. I told the agency I wanted the job if they were interested in hiring me. They were definitely interested and well, to make a long (10 year) story short, I'll skim the surface of a wonderful, peaceful 10 years.

I started work the same day as the mother's boyfriend moved in. The mother took the kids to Florida for vacation. I was there just to straighten/clean/organize the kids rooms. I didn't do housekeeping though anything that had to do with the kids I covered. The boyfriend must have thought I was a personal maid and wanted me to clean his shower. I did and he didn't like it, I wasn't a maid, just a good nanny. He wasn't nice about it and made me clean it about 5 times. After 3 days of this I got in the car very upset and cried to the kids dad. I told him I wasn't a maid, I was a nanny. "Maybe this isn't the job for me," I said. He assured me he didn't hire a maid though a nanny for his kids. He didn't care about their house being clean. He paid me for the week and let me go home until the kids got back, I was relieved.

The boyfriend left me alone from that day on. When the kids got back, we bonded and just had a fun time together. I started off working 6 days a week, the mom's house on weekdays, the dad's Friday nights and Saturdays and was off on Sundays. I did this for 6 months, though I really didn't like working with the boyfriend. So after 6 months I told their dad, it was time for me to go. He asked me why, I told him I didn't like working with the boyfriend. He then turned into The Godfather and made me an offer I couldn't refuse. He said "just work for me on weekends, Friday nights, Saturday and Sunday and I'll pay you the same amount." What a Blessing! "Do this for a year and we'll see if we're happy." he said. I had all week to do what I wanted. Only working weekends….Awesome! Wow, no boyfriend…Yes!

A happy year went by, the kids and I were very close. I felt like their big sister more than a nanny, their dad became more of a father, friend and mentor to me than an employer. Even the mother was a girlfriend, a buddy. I never clicked with the boyfriend though I didn't have to work with him so it didn't affect me anymore. After a year, I approached their dad and reminded him its been a year, Are you happy with our arrangement?" I asked. He said "Yes" "Are you?" Before I could give him a complete answer, he gave me a raise, $100 more a week. My goodness, that wasn't expected, I was just doing "happy checks" as per our original agreement. Needless to say I stayed another 3-4 years without any issues and it wasn't a job. Just weekends with my second family and I got paid for it. To this day, when people ask "What was my favorite job? I never say them as it was never a job to me, it was my second family.

I stayed a few years more without any issue. However around this time, their dad fell in love with a smart, professional psychologist, needless to say, I got nervous. A women in the house, oh boy, she would know my flaws. And she did, she was so cool, so nice, though she got on me, luckily in a loving manner. It was fine. I loved her as I did everyone else. She had 2 teenage daughters, one was 15 and the other 17. We were all one happy family, with me on weekends for all the fun activities.

As time went on I remembered my acting, I decided to put together a one woman show on my days off. I did the show at the Beverly Hills Playhouse. It was fun, I enjoyed it. This was my first chance to produce. After finishing a successful weekend with this play, I started writing and wrote a few scripts, one of which was an animated movie.

I had 9 wonderful years working for who I now call my second family. I knew it was time to leave however when the kids were driving me around. They were too old to have a nanny. Both kids now driving, I was in the car with the daughter who was now 16. We were talking about my job title, I told her "You can't say I'm your nanny anymore, just a friend of the family."

She said "Daddy said he will never fire you." Wow, this hit me hard. Its time for me to quit, I thought. I went home and cried. I knew I had to do this to make it easier for their dad. So I told him it was time for me to go on. Can you believe he gave me $10,000 as a thank you gift. Wow, unbelievable. They then hired me as personal secretary/assistant. I did that for another year, once a week. I don't think I was ever that good at personal assistant, though was willing to give it my best anyhow. I shared my money with my family as I always did, so needless to say, it went very fast.

Now 30 years old, working one day a week, living with my 2 single brothers, Derek and Jeff in Santa Monica with my youngest brother Jason now on his way to LA, I knew I wanted to move and live in peace. Three single brothers and me? Oh no,

Lord please move me out. I was praying for a peaceful surrounding,I wanted to live differently, not an apartment or a house, just different. I was thinking an Indian reservation possibly, only coming into town on weekends for my second family. I prayed God would guide me as he always did.

A few months later I picked up the house phone, it was a neighbor calling to check on us. She told me she was boat sitting. "Boat sitting?" I asked. "People live on boats?" She invited me over. I was there within 20 minutes. I walked onto the dock with this big smile on my face. "This is it, this is what I was looking for," "This is my future!" I said. She looked at me like I was crazy. Laughing, she asked, "Would you like to come in Lisa?". I told her I would be in a boat within the next few weeks…PBF.

She advised me to rent one first to make sure I liked the lifestyle. I went home right away and started looking. I found one for rent though didn't have enough to move in. The owner said I could move in now and pay him next week. I was thrilled and had a new life. A peaceful life on a boat, on the Pacific Ocean in Marina Del Rey, Ca. Thank you Lord!

CHAPTER EIGHT
SERENITY & PEACE

I was in another world, leaving the boat only on weekends to be with my second family. I loved boat life. I was in heaven. I started to be a real introvert. There was no place in the world I'd rather be than home. I lived there 6 months in peace until the boat owner started to sexually harass me.

He thought we had a chance at a relationship. I had never been sexually harassed so I didn't know how to handle it. He would tell me "I didn't have to pay rent if I'd grant him sexual favors". I made sure I paid him early so he'd leave me alone though like it usually does, it of course escalated. I would come home from a weekend with my second family and the boat would be gone. My cat, my computer, everything out at sea. He started walking in when I was sleeping, just unlocking the boat and walking in.

I was getting scared. He kept taking the boat on weekends, knowing I'm with my second family. I called the police, they were in a catch 22, he's the owner, I'm the renter. I said "if this was an apartment could he just walk in anytime he wanted too?" The police told him to leave me and the boat alone.

As long as he was renting it, he couldn't enter it. He was not driving me out of this life that I loved. I prayed and prayed. I sat on the dock late each night looking at the sky, just praying for God to get me a boat, somehow, my own boat. I started looking at boats as if the money was in my bank...PBF.

A few weeks later, I was going on my 10th year with my 2nd family, they informed me if I stayed 10 years, they would buy me a new car, put money into my one woman show or buy me a boat. Well, I didn't need a new car, I had a sports car that I got when they gave me the 10K. I didn't really want to travel with the one woman show. However a boat would be an answer to my prayers. I told them what I was going thru with my landlord. The next thing I know, they told me to go find a boat. They said, "you have $20,000 to spend and 5,000 to fix it up to live comfortable in it." I was thanking them and thanking God for working through them. I never expected that. It was never my thought that they would be part of the answer to this prayer, Wow.

I looked at a lot of boats, I had the money, Amen, though I was told when you find the right boat you will fall in love. I wasn't falling in love with any of them. Then one of my neighbors said A.V., was an Actor on the rise in between jobs at the time. This boat was on my dock though somehow I had never seen it as it was always covered. AV would come on the dock with 2-3 girls at a time and go out to the ocean, come back then cover it again.

    I left a note on his boat. He called back, so needless to say, I ran to see the boat. I stepped on it and fell in love with just the helm. It had a beautiful chestnut varnished wheel like the wheel on Gilligan's Island. The rest of the 1972 30 foot Trojan powerboat was just as beautiful. Chestnut vanished wall, white leather couches and wooden vanished floor. This boat had obviously been loved and I wanted to love it even more. Just a dream live-a-board for me. The price was $19,500, I talked him down to 17,500. That next week I was in my new home in peace and serenity… My boss and I then named the boat Full House…an answered prayer and another PBF moment.

CHAPTER NINE
HEAVEN ON EARTH

I was living in heaven and didn't go anywhere. I didn't talk to anyone, my slip fee was only $250 a month. I didn't need muh money nor did I care about having any money. I was on cloud 9. I was living my Blue Lagoon, instead of the island, I had done one step better and was living "on" the ocean. I worked one day a week for my second family until my boss's wife's sister moved to LA and took over the position. I worked 10 plus years with them. God had truly Blessed each and every one of those years.

So my job was now over and I loved home more than anywhere in the world. I wrote a few scripts and my boss taught me how to write sitcoms which he directed. I never sold anything though I didn't care, I just loved writing. I stayed very close to my second family, they helped me by having the boat varnished every year to maintain its beauty.

They occasionally paid me a visit or 2, joining me for a boat ride. I joined the coast guard auxiliary and learned to be a better captain. My few friends and family would come over every now and then and we would take the boat out. One of my neighbors hit a log in the ocean and put a hole in the bottom of his boat. That freaked me out. If that happened to my boat, I would be homeless, literally. Thats when you find out who your true friends are. "Who's taking me home with them?" I thought. So I took the boat out less and less as first and foremost, it was my home not just something I enjoyed recreationally.

To maintain it's engine, I would start it up and run it for a few minutes at least once a week. I loved the lifestyle more than going on boat rides. I thought it was so funny that the girl who introduced me to boat life was never to be seen again, after that initial day when she introduced me to my new lifestyle. I heard she moved directly there after. As many of us know, God will sometimes put someone in your path that changes it completely, and then they just vanish. She'd never saw my boat or did I ever see her again. She will always be an angel to me.

My life stopped on the boat, I was so happy, time would just pass by, weeks, months, years would pass. Just me, God and my cat Mulatto. One day I realized I hadn't talked to anyone in 2 weeks, not on the phone, not in person, nothing, just my daily conversation with God. I wasn't working and my brother Derek was paying my slip fee for that year. I had given him a lot of money over the years so he figured this was the least he could do. You'd think it would be Jeff, who enjoyed my unlimited ATM card years ago. Though when I was working and making good money, I gave all my money away. Who ever needed it, they got it. Between my siblings, Derek was the only one at that time who had given back. My brother Jason would bring me Subway sandwiches every now and then which I thought was sweet. Rainy days was buy one get one, so I had food for a few days. I was grateful and stress free. I was on the boat for about 4 years by that point. It was at this point that I knew I had to do something more with my life. Not just float away.

One night I was driving on the freeway in LA, alone, and all of sudden I felt my cousin's presence there next to me, who I had taken care of years earlier. It had been about 10 years since she died. I was so scared though I knew it was her, her presence, her spirit. I knew it was her sitting in the passenger seat of my car. The passenger side had a light, a glow and I didn't look. I just continued to look straight, needless to say, I was frightened to death.

It was then that I remembered our pact, that she would come back and visit me someday. I remember her also saying that "I would know it was her."

Well, I knew. I started pleading with her and said "I love you and I realize your here though if I look over at you while driving this car, I will die and be with you." "Please," I said, "I'm frightened, I love you though please go and I'll see you again when my time comes." From the corner of my eyes, I saw the light dim and disappear. I was so happy and so sad at the same time though I couldn't help feeling frightened. I wish I could have accepted it and to date it never happened again. I look forward to seeing her again one day in Heaven.

I was now 35 years old, celibate and my maternal clock was beginning to tick. Kids had not entered my mind for all these years, I worked with so many of them and helped raised a few of them, it just wasn't in the plans. Until someone put batteries in my clock, not Duracell batteries, just the 99 cent store batteries.

So this is what I decided, I decided to plan to backpack around the world, one ticket around the world (The World Ticket which at the time cost $2,000), getting off the plane in different countries, the ticket makes it clear that you have a year from the date you leave to get on and off the planes, starting in LA and ending in LA, always moving forward around the globe. You can go up or down to different countries though you can't go back. You must always be heading towards LA. I bought maps and started planning my dream trip, locking the boat up for a year, back packing and seeing the world.

When I got back, well, I figured my batteries would now be Duracell Maximum strength and I would go to the sperm bank and get impregnated. A man wasn't part of the plans, it wasn't my thought, a man would be a bonus. I started praying and my devotionals and discussions with God were getting much deeper. We were friends, God & I, getting closer as time went on. I spent many years with Him alone, he knew me well. I would talk with only Him for days, sometimes weeks. Always thanking Him for my life that was so good and thankful for how it was illustrated. So I told Him what I was thinking about traveling and getting impregnated. I just said "Lord you've always been there for me, You plan my trip and You guide it." I didn't ask for specifics as I usually do, just the basics of what I was looking to do.

After 15 years of having an estranged relationship with my father, thanks to a visit I had with his older sister, my Aunt Birdie in Fort Wayne, Indiana, we mended all wounds and became very close. I mentioned the idea of getting impregnated at a sperm bank to my father, who was now a pastor with his own church. "Father," I said, "I'm getting older, I've decided to take a trip around the world for a year then come back and get impregnated by the sperm bank." "What?" he said "Thats UnGodly". I explained that I wasn't doing anything wrong, no sex, just a turkey baster. Just sperm #6381402…Lol. After giving me every reason why I shouldn't do this, he finally said "I don't know how God would feel about that?" "Its too new," he said. Then he went on to say, "Get a pair of pants and just ask God to fill them." Since a man wasn't a part of my plans, I didn't do that. However I did go one huge step further than that a year later. You will learn about that in the next chapter.

I started going to a traveling seminar. It was a class on women traveling alone in Europe and Asia. At the end of that class, I walked up to the teacher, to tell him about my journey. There was a blond, curly haired girl talking with him as well, she mentioned she was a nanny. Of course that caught my attention, I pulled her to the side and told her I was also a nanny. I told her my plans. She told me that her boss, a Film Director, was filming a movie in Asia for a few months. They were looking for another nanny, she asked if I was working and if I would be interested in interviewing for the job. She added "You can make money and travel for free on your days off." Oh my goodness, another path changer. "Yes" I said, "I'm interested." I gave her my information and weeks went by. I never heard anything so I started planning my trip again. As I got back into my original idea, I forgot about the offer, weeks went by and then I get the call. "Lisa" she said "This is .Shea, the girl you met a couple weeks back at the travel seminar, the nanny, "Are you still interest in interviewing for the job?" "Yes" I said surprisingly.

Come to find out they hired someone and it didn't work out. I went to the interview, they had 4 kids, a 1 one year old and triplet 3 years olds. They had two other nannies, and a therapist for one of the triplets. Wow, I never worked with so many children or nannies. The one year old smiled at me and wanted me to hold him. It seems the one year old had hired me at that moment....another PBF. God planned this one with a bonus, a free trip and making money instead of just spending it. God is such a wonderful planner. This was so much more than I asked for, so much more than what I dreamed of. I'm glad I put it in HIS hands. I felt my life with God was indeed Heaven on Earth. It was so easy to close the boat and leave for Malaysia for 4 months. So perfectly planned.

CHAPTER TEN
THE ULTIMATE PBF

After months of being a working nanny, weekends only again, I was preparing for Asia. I decided I was going to buy refrigerator magnets everywhere I went, so when that future baby of mine cried, I'd remember I traveled before I had kids, that I had lived and lived very well, even though it was now time for a screaming baby, Lol.

We were ready to leave for Asia. Hong Kong first, then Malaysia. We lived in Malaysia for about 4 months. The boat was closed, with the advance I received, I paid the slip fee for 5 months, my cat was now with Derek and everyone was checking on the boat for me from time to time. To skim the surface, I had already bonded with the kids, the family and all the co-workers. The other two nannies and the therapist became my Malaysian sisters, we had a ball. We had a car and were driving on the opposite side of the street. The steering wheel was on the passenger side, that was a lot to get used to. We learned the basic signs and they had lots of billboards with the actress Selma Hayek on it. I guess they loved her. Well the signs guided us home. One of the other nannies found a pattern in these billboards, she said every time you see Selma say "Forget Selma" (well, she said it a little harsher) and go the other way, it actually worked. I found my way home a few times that way.

On our days off I backpacked through different parts of Asia. One of the nannies was so good at planning our schedule that I had so much time off, since I was the weekend nanny, that I could stay in Bangkok and different parts of Thailand, Singapore and backpack thru Malaysia for days at a time, 3-5 days each. Since we all had different days off, it was hard to travel together though sometimes we could if our schedules permitted. We were true bonded sisters, working together, helping each other, checking on each other when possible, dropping each other off at the bus station or airport. However we chose to travel that week.

Being with The Director of the biggest movie they've ever filmed there, we were able to stay in the King's Villa for a few weeks, it was awesome. We had butlers, maids and a personal chef. They would find out your favorite dishes and have them ready for you as soon as you walked in the door. They found out I love shrimp, crab and lobster. I swear they made a special dish with one of these shellfish daily. I fell in love with this fruit drink with mangos, papayas, pineapple and all the awesome fruit of Asia. The girls were working out each day at

Pure Blind Faith

the local gym though not me. I figured my backpacking was enough exercise. They warned me to stop drinking those high calorie fruit drinks. I figured, I don't drink, smoke or do drugs though I'm loving eating my shellfish and drinking my fruit drinks.

The butler realized I loved this drink and when I walked into the villa, he was handing this awesome fruit drink to me. It would have been insulting not to drink it...Lol. I think they wait to see when we would drive up then run to get our drinks. I went swimming one day and he brought my favorite fruit drink to me on the side of the pool. I took a sip and swam to the other side and there was another glass of it sitting there. I thought he ran it over to the other side as I swimming. I looked back and the other glass was still sitting where I left it. This was crazy, I looked at the butler and said "Please no more, thank you." Needless to say, when I got back to the states, I was 25 pounds heavier, those were happy pounds however, trust me. It was shrimp, lobster and fresh fruit pounds.

After a few months of being there, and a lot more stories, it was almost time to go home. I fell in love with the Indian culture, I loved the colors of the Indian Saris, they were so beautiful. The trip was almost over, I was down to a few hundred dollars.

Pure Blind Faith

One day I decided I wanted to get married in these beautiful Saris I saw at the Sari shop. I then went back and bought my wedding Sari, two of them (white with gold and multiply colored trim and cream with the same trim) because I couldn't decide which one I loved the most.

As I was looking at all the beautiful colored Sari's, my Pure Blind Faith popped in. I'm buying my bridesmaids Saris to match my dress. Umm… I'll probably have about 6 bridesmaids, so I bought 6 beautiful color coordinated Saris. Hot pink with Gold trimmed, Yellow with the same Gold trim, Royal Blue with Gold trim, Red with Gold trim, Green with Gold trim, and Purple with Gold trim. Then my thoughts were, "Umm…What will the guys where?" The owner showed me the shirts that the guys wore. Cream satin shirts with Crystal and Gold buttons running down the middle, beautiful, one size fits all. "Wow", I thought, "perfect!!!" "If I'm going to have six bridesmaids, its only fair that he has 6 groomsmen" I said to the shop owner. The shop owner looked at me and asked "When is the wedding? "I don't know." I said to her, "Can I have 6 of those shirts? I asked. She took a step back and looked at me puzzled. "OK" she said, looking at me like I was crazy. Maybe it was crazy in her eyes though definitely not in mine.

Pure Blind Faith

She let me know that traditionally Indian women wear red on their wedding day. I thanked her for the information and said, "That's ok, Americans wear white or cream, I brought both". I looked at her and asked again, What do the kids wear to a traditional Indian wedding? She looked puzzled. I have 3 little nephews around 1 or 2 years old. She showed me these beautiful satin suits for little boys. By the time I get married they will be about 3 to 5 years old. I'll buy 4 of those suits for 4-5 years olds" I said. "Whoever my husband will be might have a nephew too." I thought. "OK," she said in disbelief. I bought 2 extra saris for 2 flower girls and I thought, "I'll let my husband pick his own suit." I said. She said "Oh you're engaged?" "No," I said "I don't even have a boyfriend." She laughed and so did I. I walked out with my whole wedding party, spending the last dollars I had. I walked away however with a lot of excitement.

I was so excited to show my Malaysian sisters and my boss, the mom of the kids, what I bought for my entire wedding party based on faith. Little did I know it would be the bulk and punchline to every joke in the house. The questions came and wouldn't stop. "Are you crazy?" "You spent all your money on this?' "Does a groom come with this wedding?" "You don't even have a boyfriend?" "When is the wedding?" " You might have to walk down the aisle alone Lisa." "What will you do if your nephew are 10-11 years old?" They won't be." I said with a lot of confidence. There was a lot of head shaking and disbelief going on. You would have thought I just built Noah's Ark. Then one of the nannies said, "Lisa, what if your husband doesn't like this?" "Have you thought of that?" "No I didn't, though any man that I marry will be as colorful as these Saris, he'll love it." as I smiled confidently. I left the Saris out and stared at it all night, smiling and thanking God for them. As we packed to go home I heard comments in the house like "Did Lisa pack her wedding party?" "Yeah, though she forgot the Groom!" That was funny, everyone laughed, even I laughed. I realized in their minds I just built Noah's Ark. In my mind I just sealed my future, my fate. Now looking back it was the Ultimate PBF. Though remember, I was blind to my Blind Faith. I was just doing as I always did. If you pray for something God will answer it and I'm living as if it already happened. There was no doubt in my mind this would happen sooner than later.

CHAPTER ELEVEN
LOVE@AOL.COM

So now we're back in LA. I was excited to see my cat though sad to go home to my lonely life. When I got back, I still worked for them on weekends. I ended out working for them for 2 years. During that time I was on the boat, back to my life though becoming very lonely. I decided to go back to my original plan, to backpack around the world then get impregnated. Now I'm working and will save up for the ticket and start planning the trip. I have some experience backpacking now and the travel bug was biting me big time. I couldn't get anyone to go with me, my girlfriends were very much into they daily lives. So I decided to plan it alone though I thought it would be fun having someone to email and share my thoughts and journey with. I answered single ads in the local Marina's paper and went on quite a few dates, mostly first dates only. My date spot was The Cheesecake Factory in Marina Del Rey. It was walking distance from the boat and far enough that no one knew were the boat was.

It was crazy. I met a nerd, a philosopher, a Mr. Hollywood "I think I'm a superstar" type, a surfer dude and who can forget the momma's boys. I had two different guys ask to take me to meet their mother, "Your the kind of girl my mother always wanted me to meet." they said. Well, I thought, "I don't like her son, why meet the mother." Needless to say, they never heard from me again after saying that. I had a white guy tell me I wasn't black enough for him, he wanted to be someones "Boo". "What's a BOO?" I asked. "See" he said, "You act too white." I had a black guy ask me, "How can you live on a boat, black people can't swim?" "I was also told I had a baby face, he wanted a woman, not a baby." I thought if I could have a baby face at 36 years old, then hey, thats a blessing.

I went on 4 dates with one guy, two at The Cheesecake Factory, one at another nearby restaurant. After a few dates, I agreed to get in the car with him and go to The House of Blues @Universal studios. During that date, he expressed how much he liked me and was thinking we should get a boat together. "Really?" I said in disagreement. He was mixed like me, black and white. He was nice enough for a few dates though nothing was developing for me, no feelings. The music started playing and he got up to dance. I don't know if he was nervous or what, though he started dancing all over the place, saying "excuse me" to everyone he hit, side swiped and ran into everyone on the dance floor.

Pure Blind Faith

He danced like he was drunk though had never had a drink. I was so turned off after this date.

So how do you get rid of a nice guy you ask? Ask him for money. The next time he called I told him I couldn't go out with him as I was going through a lot. I told him I needed $5,000 to get through it. He got off the phone after wishing me luck. The next week he called to check on me, we talked and I asked if he had $5,000 that he could give me, not lend me. Needless to say our conversations got shorter and further apart. The last call I was still going through my issue so that was a 2 minute conversation. I never heard from him again after that. I got rid of him in 3 calls in 3 weeks. As far as he felt, he got rid of me....Amen, no stalker here. Thank God.

Since all my one time dates were at The Cheesecake Factory, all the waitresses began to know me by name. One day one of the waitresses asked me if I liked any of the guys I've dated. "We always see you walk home after," she said. I told her my secret, if they're a good date or a nice guy, I order a California Omelette which was $7. If its a bad date who's boring or self centered, talks too much or wants me to meet his mother right off the bat, well then I order Shrimp Scampi which was $15. At least I'm going to eat well on a bad date. She laughed. The next date I was on, another waitress I knew came up to me with a smirk on her face, "Hi Lisa, what will you be having tonight?" I can see the waitress I told my secret to and two other waitresses laughing, waiting for my answer. "Shrimp Scampi" I said politely. When that waitress walked back, I heard a lot of laughing. With all my dating, I didn't meet anyone special. I gave up. I mean, let's face it, I enjoyed my own company on the boat and eating alone seemed more peaceful at the time.

Shortly there after as I was planning my adventure, I decided to put an ad on love@aol.com as I planned my journey. I mean hey, what did I have to lose, it was free, easy and I could delete the riff-raff. My profile picture was of me and my nephew (a baby). I figured if any man got turned off by the picture with me holding a baby, then he need not apply. I titled it, " A Good woman for a Good man." I added that I was looking for someone to share beautiful rainstorms with. I loved hearing the rain hit the boat, it was so tropical. I had my crazy rules:

1. If the email was too long, 2-5 pages or more (once it was 10 pages), he needed to get a life. He's as lonely as I was, probably weird....Delete.

2. If it's too short, he doesn't really care and is probably tired of typing different women on the net....Delete

3. If it's too basic, its a basic letter he sends to everyone... Delete

4. If he didn't capture me in the first 2 lines... Delete

Well, needless to say, I deleted most of them. Once in a while I would email someone back, then they'd email me back once or twice, then it died. Eight months of emails about 5 new emails each day. Then a kindergarten teacher emailed me. I thought, he loves kids, he's a Kindergarten teacher. We emailed back and forth then set a date to meet. In his picture he had an okay face with a bodybuilder type body. I'm not a big fan of that look as in my experience it usually spelled insecurity or cockiness. However, I said Hey, he's a Kindergarten teacher," he can't be that bad. We shared some nice emails and had nice conversations. Well, not long after, we met at none other than The Cheesecake Factory of course. To my surprise, he looked like a geek, I mean, super geek, excuse me...Urkel. I said, "That was not your body in the picture." He laughed and said "No, it wasn't, he put his face on someone else's body." That told me a lot, he's a liar and obviously very insecure. He obviously uses that picture just to lure girls onto dates in hopes they'd like him enough at that point to see past all that. Really? What's the point? Needless to say, I had Shrimp Scampi and never spoke with him again.

I was so frustrated. I started praying, "Lord, do you have any one out there for me?" "All the people in the world and no one for me?" Really? I threw my wallet on the floor with about twenty pictures fell out of it. "Lord is he in my wallet? Have I met him?
What's his name? All I saw was pictures of kids, lots of kids. the triplets with Santa, couples with their kids, nieces, nephews, I thought, "he's not here, only kids."

"OK Lord, I'm going to break down for you what I'm looking for." I said.

I then told God exactly what I was looking for:

1. Olive skin, dark hair and dark eyes. God, I would love someone who looks like Jesus, someone in your son's image. Since you picked that look, I'll go for that look.

2. I desired someone who was a bit overweight so he could understand me being overweight as well.

3. He can be in show business, like everyone I was around. However I desire him to be the type that doesn't go to the parties or feels the need to be around all the Hollywood garbage.

4. I desired someone who would enhance me, enhance my happiness. I'm already happy just lonely.

5. He had had to know and love you God.

6. He had to be fun, witty, interesting, romantic and creative.

7. He had to be different than other guys. Stand out as unique.

8. He had to love his Mother, so he knew how to respect a woman.

9. He had to love boat life, just as I did.

I had no reason to settle for less than I desired, I had a good life, plus God had spoiled me over the years giving me all that I prayed for. I wanted someone that I could share beautiful rainstorms with. I loved hearing the rain fall on the boat. So I was willing to wait or live without for as long as God wanted me too.

For years I didn't have any interest in a man or partner, just kids since my maternal clock was ticking even stronger now. So I thought, well, maybe the sperm bank was best idea at this point. Then I had to think of what my father said "Get a pair of pants and ask God to fill them." I couldn't bring myself to do that, buying diapers made more sense I thought. I let go of the idea of meeting anyone and concentrated on my trip along with my research on the sperm bank.

Two weeks later, I got an email from a guy. The email was about 10 lines and was titled "a Romantic Rainstorm." It was short, interesting and sweet. He was a Filmmaker from Boston named Daryl. The picture he attached was handsome and he was holding a camera. He loved some of the same movies I loved. I excitingly emailed him back. He emailed me back shortly there after. This went on for 3 weeks sometimes 3 to 4 times a day. I said to myself, "Well, he's in Boston," so of course I felt I could be open and free to talk to this guy since he's 3,000 miles away. The emails got better and better and more intense.

After 3 weeks he instant messages me, he mentions that he had a long day at work. I asked, "Oh wow, what did you do? He said "I worked security today for the Oscars." I asked, "The Oscars!!!" "Oscars?" "That's in LA?" I was shocked and I sounded it I'm sure. "Yes I live here." he said. "I thought you lived in Boston?" I asked. "No, I'm from Boston though I live in LA." Oh my goodness, I didn't want to meet this guy, I just wanted to enjoy his emails. We instant messaged each other for about 3 hours, then he said "Are you tired of typing? I'd like to call you, let's talk by phone. I got nervous, butterflies nervous. I then asked "How about I call you?" So I called him and blocked my number. We talked for at least 3 or 4 hours and after that conversation, I had a date. It was very apparent by that conversation there was chemistry. That was on a Tuesday, our date was Friday. I was nervous all week. I was hoping he wasn't like the kindergarten teacher. I emailed him to confirm and asked "Do you look like your picture? "Yes," he said, "that's me." He then asked, "Do you look like your picture?" I of course answered "Yes." "Well, then you have nothing to worry about." He said. Thru email, I was also talking to a chef from

Hawaii who was working in Beverly Hills. I wasn't as open to meeting him, I knew he was in LA though I didn't feel as connected. The chef asked for a date, I thought, should I see him Thursday and then see Daryl on Friday? Therefore I wouldn't be disappointed with the guy I opened myself up too, Daryl. There's no disappointment with the Chef, I didn't open up to him. I couldn't bring myself to confirm with the chef. "Next week" I told him, I'm having a busy week at the moment.

Needless to say, I had the longest week of my life. I did and I didn't want to meet Daryl. I just wanted to receive emails from him. Friday night then came, 9:00pm, of course at The Cheesecake Factory. I sat on the bench outside the restaurant nervous, I wasn't prepared to meet this guy, I told him so much about myself, he called around 8:45pm to tell me he would be about 5 minutes late. Wow that's cool, how respectful, I thought. Most guys just show up 5 minutes late like its no big deal.

March 31st, 2000, it was now 9:05pm. Daryl gets out of the car wearing all black, a black jacket, black shirt and black pants. He was Italian, Lebanese with a little Portuguese. He had dark hair, dark eyes with olive skin, the first thing on my checklist. He had this big smile on his face. I was thinking "Wow, he looks just like his picture." A little overweight though carried it well, definitely no nerd nor did he carry himself like a cocky Hollywood Director. He looked humble and secure. We walked into the restaurant, instead of sitting inside the restaurant like I usually would, we went out to the bonfire. My waitress friend came up to us and said "What would you be having today Lisa, a California Omelette or Scampi?" She was waiting for my usual answer. Though I answered, "nothing." She was surprised and asked "nothing? He didn't order anything either.

We just started talking at the bonfire, my name was then announced over the loud speaker at the restaurant. Daryl looked at me and asked, "Are they calling you?" "Yes" I answered. I figured it was the waitress calling to see if I was okay. It was my friend who I called my sister that was staying on the boat with me for a few days. She told me she had a flat tire around the corner and needed my Triple A card. I told her I didn't drive, I walked.

She asked if my date could bring me to her. "I just met him" I don't get in the car with guys I just met. "Are you crazy?" I asked. "Please" she said, "I need help." I then went back to the bonfire, Daryl asked "Is everything okay?" I told him what happened to my sister/friend. He didn't hesitate, "let's go get her" he said. My head was spinning, I was going against all my dating rules. I was now in the car with this guys I opened my life too. I told him the directions to where she was, turn right, turn left, go straight.

He followed all of my directions, so I guess he wasn't looking to kill me. We arrived to where she was waiting and called Triple A, the car got towed and she asked if Daryl could take her back to the boat. I'm debating with her at this point saying, "I never let anyone know where the boat is." He offered to drive her home, she said "I'm going to the boat." I'm fuming by this point. She's breaking all my rules.

Now he knows where the boat is. We didn't have a date yet though he knows where the boat is now. We decided to go to the end of the street to talk at a park bench overlooking the ocean. She calls and says, "I want to order a pizza, how do I give the address to the boat?" I'm telling her the address, he's listening, oh, by this point I am so mad with her.
Now not only does he know where it is though now has the address. I turned my phone off in case she decided to call back. The chemistry is amazing,

even better than it was when we emailed each other or talked on the phone. He obviously felt it as well as he boldly though romantically kissed me. I've never kissed ANYONE of the first date. It felt right, if felt natural, wow, I'm having such a great time. We talked until 2am, I had to work my weekend nanny job that next morning so he ended it with "I'll call you." That was one of the best dates I ever had. Though will he call again I thought? Ever? Will I see this guy again? I tell you, God definitely orchestrated that whole evening to take me out of my routine and most importantly, my comfort zone.

The next morning, one of the new nannies told everyone at work, I had a special date last night and told them how nervous I was. So when I got to work everyone was asking about my date. I had been on plenty of dates and never talked about any of them. I found myself talking about him. He's a Director I said. My boss then looked at me and said "Oh, He's trying to get to me." I looked at him and boldly expressed, "He doesn't even know who I work for, all he knows is I'm a nanny."

Well anyhow, I told them for the first time I broke all my dating rules. My heart was hoping to hear from him again. Guys usually play the game of waiting out a week or two, so I'll wait it out. Usually I don't care if they call back or not. For the first time, I cared. Preparing to wait a week, I get a call from him that afternoon saying how much he enjoyed our date and that he would like to see me again. "Within 24 hours, he called, thats a record," I thought excitingly. It also told me he's not one of those game players that has to wait a week or 2 to show interest. He doesn't live by those rules. The chef then called me for a date. I told him I met someone special that I really like therefore I wasn't interested in going out with him any longer.

He couldn't believe I would go out on a first date with a guy and cancel all others. "Who does that?" he asked. I know it sounds crazy though if I went out with you after meeting him, I would feel like I was cheating on him." I said. "Its crazy, its just something about him." "I wish you went out with me first," he said. "God works in mysterious ways," I implied. I don't think he was trying to hear all that. Obviously his ego was a little bruised though I wasn't worried about that at all. All I could think was Wow, little did I know how my life would change on love@aol.com.

CHAPTER TWELVE
"THE ONE!!!"

From our first date, Daryl and I had been seeing each other every Monday. He was awesome and I was starting to like him a lot. I didn't know if this was the guy God had sent to me though he had a lot on my checklist including being a bit overweight. I thought, let me find out more about this guy before I fall in love, which I had never done with anyone. If he's dating me on Monday, I thought hey, who is he dating Tuesday through Sunday? So I created a fake email address, a name and started to email him as this girl, Keisha 24. I knew he liked ethnic girls, 24's a good age too I thought, I'm a lot older, 36.

I told him our paths crossed, Keisha's path that is, a while ago and I'd love to go to dinner with him. I sent him a picture of another girl, a pretty young girl. Seeing if he'd take the bait. Keisha emailed about 5 times, he never answered any of the emails. I was wondering if he wasn't getting the email? After a few weeks of nice Keisha's letters, Keisha, well, I, was getting frustrated. Then I remembered, if he really likes me, he shouldn't be answering Keisha. I forgot why I was doing it and was focusing on Keisha. After 2 months of dating him, I ended out confessing Keisha to him. He said, "Wow, was that you?" I asked "Why didn't you answer Keisha?" He said "Why would I answer her, I had no interest in her, I'm dating you." "Wow, good answer," I thought.

Then he goes on to say, "I'd like to see you more by the way, I notice your ad is still on Love@aol.com." "You can take your ad off and consider yourself taken," he said lovingly. My heart dropped. I always wanted a guy to say that, though of course it had to be the right guy. We fell deeply in love with each other. Together all the time, madly in love, we were the kissing and hugging type. I still worked weekends and he wrote while I was at work. We went on cruises together and did a lot the first few months. I stopped planning my trip around the world.

He asked me to stop talking about the sperm bank. He said "If things work out, I am your sperm bank." Wow, God's bonus, a father for my kids. We went to visit Derek who lived 2 hours away from LA. Derek said "Does he know you have your whole wedding party in my closet?" "No," I said. "I totally forgot about it." "Don't tell him, he might run away plus he asked me to let go of the sperm bank idea, so I did."

We started dating exclusively. I asked him if he would like to move onto the boat with me. He agreed and felt it was the right time as well. I took him to meet the rest of my family and my second family. When my father met Daryl AKA "Babe," he said "That boy is going to be a preacher one day." We both laughed. My second family said "Stick by that man Lisa, he's going places." I then met Babe's family in Boston over the phone. His sisters said" Your the one!!!" We were only together a few months so this took me back. Then he told me his mother was coming out to LA for a week or 2 to visit. "It's time to meet my mother," he said. I always ran from that one though for the first time I embraced it. "OK," I said.

Things were different with this guy, I broke all my rules, actually I had no more crazy rules, I just went with the flow. Then I get a call, one of my girlfriends was on tour with Musical Artist Macy Gray. She said Macy was looking for a nanny for her 3 kids. My girlfriend recommended me. I would go on tour with her for a year if I accepted the job offer. I told my girlfriend I think I found "THE ONE." I was ready to leave my weekend job, I love them though it was almost time to move on, its been 2 years though to now go on tour for a year… umm, I didn't know what to do.

If I didn't go and we break up, I will regret my decision. If I go, we might fall apart and go our separate ways. I, of course prayed and put it in God hands. A few weeks later God answered my prayers. Macy cancelled her tour. I didn't have to make a choice. I was free to continue our relationship. I was so excited, we both were. I quit my job though one of my Malaysian sisters offered me a job with her new boss, another director. During my time working with my new boss. he Won an Oscar, It was exciting watching it on TV with his toddler twins, hearing them say "Dada, Mama" to the TV when they saw their parents on the red carpet. I got to hold my first Oscar and Babe took a picture with it, which I know is another PBF. That boss looked at me and said, "Lisa, Daryl reminds me myself when I was younger as an up and coming director." I had a lot of confirmation that I made a good choice in both the man God chose for me and in supporting his talent. I had a new job, a new man and my happiness was enhanced.

Then I bleached the twins expensive new onesie accidentally. I was so mad at myself. My new job I just made a big mistake. So I laid the onesie on the couch on display to show my boss when they got home. When they walked in, I apologized and told them to take it out of my pay. The twins mom said,"Lisa it looks like clouds, looks cool to me." Then she said, "Lisa most people put in back in the drawer and we have to figure out what happened." I told her that I would never let someone else get blamed for something I did. I expressed that my honesty get me in trouble sometimes. "How can honesty get you in trouble?" she expressed. "Honesty can get you in as much trouble as a lie can," I said. Well, I didn't have to pay for it and they admired my honestly.

One day Daryl and I were talking and he mentioned he played Santa at the Beverly Hills mall the previous Christmas season. I mentioned that the kids I was nannying had taken a picture with Santa at the mall during that season. I then pulled out the picture and Wow, there he was, Daryl as Santa in my wallet with the triplets and the baby. I got teary eyed and I told him I had thrown my wallet on the floor and asked God if the man for me was in my wallet. It was all kids, the only man was Santa and it was you, Wow!

My brother Derek didn't believe it at first and asked to see the picture. After looking at it, he was stopped in his tracks and said "Wow, it is him." Another gift God gave Babe is a great memory with lots of details. Babe said "Wow, I remember your boss, she had triplets and a baby that cried for his mom to be in the picture though she didn't want to be in the picture." "She also had 2 nannies with her, a straight haired white girl, which was the new girl and a spanish girl, I don't remember you however," he said." I wasn't there, it was my day off." I expressed with amazement. One of those nannies was one of my Malaysian sisters and the other was the new girl. Wow, another unbelievable PBF moment.

We had many moments like that, many things in common, my goodness, my checklist was getting smaller and smaller. We were both the 2nd of 5 children, we both caught the bouquet at the last wedding we were at, we both kept a list of names for our children in our notebooks, some of the same names, mostly earthly names. Babe had always signed his cards "Peace, Love & God Bless." Two of the middle names of our children. He also had a friend, a spiritual advisor he befriended. She told him he would meet a unique woman that lived on or around water. She also said that the one movie they saw together with mutual friends was a movie I was associated with somehow. It was indeed the same movie I was in Malaysia for...Wow!!! He showed me the email where she wrote all of this. I was just amazed at how God orchestrates both the events and the people in our life.

The day came and I met Babe's mom. The first thing I humbly said to her was "I'm 10 years older than your son and I'm black, white and Native American, do you have a problem with this?" She said, "Are you kidding, not at all." She and I hit it off from that point on. We had a ball in LA. She had a lot of fascinating characteristics and was different than any woman I had met. Beautiful, Unique, fun, classy, hard language at times though a very generous person.

Daryl and his mom had a special bond, almost like siblings or best friends. Another thing off of my checklist. She wanted to look at houses in LA. We were in this beautiful house, I looked at Babe and said, "Wouldn't you want a house like this?" He thought about it for a moment then said, "I'd rather have a bigger boat." My heart melted and I knew at that moment, he was "The One." That was the last thing on my checklist in Chapter 11.

Shortly there after, we did our first production together, a play for my grandparents 80th birthday. We called it "Vinnie and Maude." The title was based on my grandparents middle names. Babe wrote it, It was fun, creative and witty. Everyone loved it, laughed at the jokes and reacted to the different recreated characters of 1920, Henry Ford, Betty Boop and the Andrew Sisters. I enjoyed performing with him, he was great to bounce off of... what a blast.

On my first birthday that I shared with Babe, he Won an award for a short film he filmed in both Boston & LA shortly before we met. I was so excited to share that with him on my birthday. The fact that it happened to fall on my birthday was pretty awesome. On his first birthday together in November, I surprised him with his first cruise. It was so much fun having someone to enjoy things with, a true partner, that I was in love with.

Our first Christmas, we got Santa hats, decorated the boat and even bought matching Christmas pajamas which was the beginning of a lifetime of matching outfits. I bought a 3 foot tree to put our gifts under. I bought a wooden family train and I put each of my siblings and their spouses name on a train and their kids name in a star that was attached to the train. I did a train for Daryl and I and bought 2 little stars for our train then attached the whole family together to make a long train. When I gave it to Derek to keep on the family tree, he said "Why did you buy 2 extra stars for your train?" "Thats our 2 children," I said with confidence...PBF. I had the best Christmas ever that year. I had someone I loved to share it with.

Two months later, we went on a cruise during Valentine's week, that morning Babe gave me a talking red bear that he recorded his voice on. It said, "Happy Valentine's Day Lisa Willice Goggins, I Love You." We exchanged gifts, chocolates and went on with our fabulous day. Evening came and we went back to the room to get ready for dinner.

Babe was in the bathroom, there was a note next to the Valentine bear saying "Press me again." This time the bear said "Lisa Willice Goggins, will you marry me?" I fell to the floor crying. I had been proposed to 4 times in my life though this time it was right. Of course, for the first time I said "YES!!!" At that point we were together for 11 months. He said "I wanna be able to tell our children we were engaged within a year." I went into the bathroom, I prayed and cried and prayed and cried again. God had truly answered everything on my checklist, all my prayers, my kids would have a father, a fun father and I would have a husband that I was madly in love with a bonus, he loved boat life. My journey was complete. I now had someone to share romantic rainstorms with. Wow God, Daryl is truly "THE ONE." Thank you.

CHAPTER THIRTEEN
PBF AT WORK

We still had a few days on the cruise ship, I was glowing. I couldn't wait to tell everyone I was engaged. We planned our wedding date and the kind of wedding we wanted, a musical, a show on a cruise ship, another production. Now I was able to tell him about the wedding party Saris I bought in Malaysia, including the men's shirts. He was so excited and looking forward to seeing all the colors. When I took him to see them, he loved them, all of them. He said, "I have to get a suit to match them." I remember saying that years ago to the shop owner, so of course I laughed. We found the Indian community in LA after planning the wedding, we ended up with 12 bridesmaids and 12 groomsmen, double than what I brought back. God's bonus again. So the Indian shop got 6 more shirts for us. I let six girls pick from the original Saris and 6 girls got new ones from the shop. I wanted the original Saris back. Those who wanted to keep their Saris got new ones.

We wanted to do creative invitations, something different, so we got very innovative with it. We bought 200 Orange Crush hour glass shaped soda bottles. We poured the soda out, got sand from the beach, lots of small seashells, scroll looking paper and 200 rectangular boxes for the bottles. We put together a message in a bottle with all the cruise ship, hotel and wedding information. It was a lot of work though very fun. He was just as excited and into it as I was. Even some family members got involved and helped.

Shortly afterwards, Babe and I sat on the beach one day talking about kids. We agreed on discipline and upbringing. We named our children and agreed to stop when we had a boy and a girl. We had 2 boys names and 2 girls names and little did we know at that time that they would come in the order we named them.

Soleil Love
Ocean Peace
Heavenlee Joy
River Peace

As the wedding day approached, we of course had to get legally married before getting on the cruise ship and having our wedding show on international waters as this wouldn't have counted as a legal wedding. I told Babe I didn't care what day we had the legal wedding, I said surprise me if you'd like.

He's great at being spontaneous anyway. Weeks later, he told me we had a meeting with the travel agency that was helping us with all the cruise details. As we were heading towards the meeting near my brother's house, Babe went the wrong direction on the freeway. As far as I knew, we were already late for the meeting so of course I was a little upset with him for going in the wrong direction. I went to call the agency, gladly, he then stopped me and revealed we were going to Las Vegas to get legally married.

"Today's your Wedding day, July 31, 2001" he said. I was so surprised, two weeks before we had our cruise ship wedding. I, of course started crying, I was overjoyed. We get to Las Vegas and drive into the parking lot of The Viva Las Vegas Wedding Chapel. He had arranged a mobster wedding with a mobster theme room. He then told me the wedding would be live on the Internet for anyone who wanted to watch it as it happened. Wow, how unbelievable and creative, especially for the year 2001. The significance of the mob themed wedding would come up later in life.

The cruise line told us we could use their main theatre for our 4 musical acts if we had 60 guests and already legally married. We were Blessed to have 90 guests, 45 on each side of the family. The day before, as the guests arrived, we had a Bon Voyage party for the guests going on the cruise and for all who weren't able to make it on the cruise as well. Everyone that desired too, had the opportunity to make a speech. My Malaysian sisters told the story of the Saris, they were in disbelief that 2 years later we'd be wearing those Saris. My nephew were 4-5 years old as I visioned and he had a 3 year old nephew and they all actually fit into the suits. My father got up and told the story of the pants and asking God to fill them, even though I didn't do it. He said he prayed for God to do it for me. Everyone that knew me had the same speech, "We never thought Lisa would get married. She was so happy and content on the boat. We couldn't get her off the boat." That speech was made about 15 times.

The next day, we happily boarded the cruise ship with our 90 guests. The cruise ship of course checked to assure we were legally married before heading into international waters. They called our wedding a mock wedding, not a real wedding for legal purposes. Babe and I didn't care what they called it, we knew it was our "real" wedding. Our 4 musical acts were awesome with our bridesmaids and groomsmen dancing. Babe had choreographed each of the acts except for one. Act 1 was my story which included the saris, this one was choreographed by an Indian Choreographer. Act 2 was Babe's story. The girls in this one were Babe's sisters who did a Lebanese dance. They were then joined by the guys who did an Italian dance. Act 3 was Babe and I dancing to a medley of love songs. Act 4 was the wedding ceremony which included a beautiful entrance by both the bridesmaids and groomsmen. My father ministered over the wedding ceremony. Babe and I had the best three days of our life. According to everyone else, so did they. Parties, lobster, cakes and just pure fun. Wow, once again, PBF at work.

CHAPTER FOURTEEN
TIME TO GIVE UP

When we got off the boat, the next day I received a call from my boss. They didn't make it to my wedding, I had only worked for them 6 months. They asked me to go to Seattle with them the next day. I had family in town so naturally I didn't want to go. I just got off the ship however I felt obligated. I mean, after all, it was my job. In Seattle, I couldn't understand why I was there and not one of my other Malaysia sisters/bridesmaids, especially one in particular. I was the weekend nanny now stuck in Seattle for a week. I was so depressed and so busy I didn't even have a chance to call my husband as often as I would have liked. I haven't even introduce him as my husband. One of my co-workers/bridesmaids called and asked me "Why are you in Seattle and not me?" I didn't know. She's the full-time nanny, I'm part time, weekends, so it was a bit odd to me as well.

The next day they told me they decided to fire her, she was costing too much. I was so hurt by this. When I spoke with her the next day, I put myself in her shoes. If it was me I would be upset if she didn't tell me this bad news. She said again, "I don't get why your there and not me?" "Do you know why?" This time I did knew why, I had to tell the truth, so sadly I told her, "They're firing you.". Understandably, she was very upset. She called her agency upset and they of course then called our boss.

The next day, one of my bosses and her assistant asked me if I told my friend she was getting fired, I of course told them the truth. Honesty getting me in trouble. I said, "Yes I did." With the advice of my boss's assistant, who sadly lied quite a bit, especially to our employer, I was then fired as well. The assistant said "Lisa's honesty and commitment should be to her boss not the help. I let them know that my honesty and commitment doesn't have a social ladder, its for everyone, rich or poor." So I was fired with much respect. I guess you would call it, fired with honor. I found out later, the father, my other boss was very upset at my firing. I heard he said "I was the most honest person in the house."

I had never been fired before so I was understandably hurt. However, God Blessed my honesty. Two weeks later I learned I was pregnant and my employers didn't fight my unemployment. I was making nearly as much unemployed as I was employed. I got to enjoy my pregnancy, stress free, with an income and my new husband on the boat who was bringing in an income as well thru film/video work. That was my last nanny job, I was now to become a permanent nanny, a mom, Amen, PBF...

Three months later, Babe arranged our honeymoon, another cruise, this time out of Miami, Florida. We snorkeled the deep ocean together which was amazing and now I was 4 months pregnant and thrilled. I prayed that God give us a healthy little girl with Babe's Italian long thick hair.

We needed a bigger boat, our boat was too small for a baby. We looked in faith for another boat. We found a 1969 Tri-level Owen Aruba, we prayed that God would grant us this boat. This time I called my second family, if we sell Full house and give them the money for that sale, would they buy the new boat for us. They agreed, Amen, we were Blessed to have a new boat named Hakuna Matata (no worries).

I was enjoying my marriage, pregnancy and new life. Babe was starting to get more work doing music videos and other film projects. I followed him back and forth from Boston to LA. It was easy to close the boat and leave for months at a time when necessary. I did most of my prenatal care in Boston.

Pure Blind Faith

Babe and I agreed that when it was time to give birth it would be in LA. My dreams of having a California baby was answered on May 31st, 2002, our first baby girl was born, Soleil Love, 9 lbs, 7 oz. Soleil was going to be a water birth though due to her being breech and my gestational diabetes, it didn't happen. It was a planned C-section, we even got to pick her birth date. I walked in pregnant and walked out with a baby. No labor pain and no contractions, just recovery from surgery. In the recovery room, I was so restless and anxiously awaiting to see my baby girl. I was moving around in the bed to make the numbness go away. I was fighting the medicine to wear off. The doctor made me stop. Its been 3 hours, I wanted to be with Soleil. Finally it wore off and they wheeled me to my room and there she was, my beautiful baby Soleil Love. Wow, what an amazing experience that was.

We were thrilled. Taking Soleil home to the boat to start her life as a mermaid. We were thrilled to raise our daughter in that beautiful lifestyle. My boss that fired me sent us a big basket of pink items and clothes from The Pottery Barn. I was truly fired with honors. My second family agreed to be the Godparents. Unemployment had run out by this point though we were okay. Babe's sister had temporarily moved to Orlando, Florida. So after 2 months we were on the plane to Orlando for a week and then on the road again filming music videos around the country, mostly in LA, Boston & Buffalo.

One day, I took some paper dolls and created a picture of a mother, a father and a little girl holding her doll and a little boy. Soleil was only a few months old. My mother visited us on the boat one day, saw the picture and said "Who's the picture of?" I said, "my family." She then said, "Who's the little boy in the picture?," I said "Ocean." She asked if I was pregnant? I said "no, but that's the way I picture my family." She said "What if Ocean was another girl?" I said he won't be though if so, I'll put a pink ribbon on the little boys head. Well, needless to say, this was another PBF moment. Remember I was blind to my Blind Faith so I didn't think of it at the time as PBF.

Life was so good though of course when life is at a beautiful place, here comes the enemy to try and seek and destroy. I was grateful to be home with Soleil 24/7 wherever we were USA. As a wife, I was very happy though also a bit worried that Babe would answer to the call of temptation and get involved with the adult film industry where he had a couple acquaintances. They were suggesting he could make good money by doing adult film work.

You know, a little work for big money. I was pulling him right, though, that temptation, was pulling left. There was some tug of war going on. I prayed and prayed for God to bring him work. Babe was indeed getting more work, music videos, commercials, pilot sitcoms, mostly in Boston, some in Buffalo and I was happy. I felt I had definitely won the porn war. Thank God Babe's Holy spirit was more powerful than his dark spirits. Babe was also documenting our life on the road.

After Soleil was 9 months old, we decided to have another child. I then said to God, "Wow, you did so well with Soleil, how about a challenge to top yourself with Ocean?" Soleil so beautiful and perfect. Give Ocean something Soleil doesn't have and special mark that represents you. Wow, he definitely did just that. It took almost 2 years to get pregnant again. We tried and tried to the point where we were ready to spend what it took to make this happen. We were going to get fertility treatments and before we started the pills they tested me for pregnancy, it happened, Wow, I was now pregnant with our little boy...PBF Again! God is so good. Doing prenatal in Boston, we still agreed he would be born in LA so naturally we flew back to LA a month or 2 beforehand. I was scheduled to give birth on March 6th. Babe was scheduled to film a music video and had the option to do it either before the birth or after. I preferred he do it before so he would be there to help with Soleil after our son was born, he agreed and flew back to Boston a couple weeks before the due date.

So three weeks before Ocean's scheduled C-section date, he left for Boston for a week. I went to my midwife that helped me through my pregnancy with Soleil and she arranged everything for me. I dropped Soleil at my sister, Jennifer's house and went for my appointments. At the doctors office, they were disputing me over the pregnancy weeks, I said 34 weeks, they said 38 weeks. He wasn't due until March 6th, it was February 22nd, I had a few weeks, they didn't agree. I wanted a natural birth since I had a C-section with Soleil. They told me I couldn't have a natural birth after a C-section. I had been praying to feel what a contraction or labor pain felt like since I didn't feel anything with Soleil and I knew this would be my last baby.

After all my testing, I picked up Soleil at my sister's house and headed home. I was at the drive thru of In & Out burger and all of a sudden I felt a big jolt in my stomach, I hurried home. It took me twenty minutes to get from the parking lot to the boat dock, which normally takes 2 minutes. I was doubled over in pain. Soleil now 2 1/2 years old was assisting me saying "Mommy please walk, mommy please." I made it to the boat and the pain got worse. I was in labor, and boy did I feel the labor pains. Babe was coming home the next day, that evening at 10 pm. I was in so much pain that Soleil begged me to stop screaming. I didn't want to tell anyone because I knew they would rush me to the hospital and give me a C-section and babe would miss the birth of his son. I felt it would have been my fault since I talked him into leaving before the birth instead of after.

Soleil was amazing thru this process and rubbed my tummy saying "Mommy, don't worry, you'll feel better." I didn't tell anyone, only Babe. I labored all night, screaming all night with Babe on the phone trying to comfort me and pray me thru it. He asked me if I felt I should go to the hospital? Not wanting him to miss the birth, I said no. That morning some brown stuff started coming out of me. I was scared it could be blood, so I called my sister and told her. I asked her to call the doctor for me, not give my name though ask what could this be. The doctor told her that the mother must be checked to make sure the baby was okay. I'm crying, "Babes not here, I can't have Ocean without Babe."

At 10 am, my midwife called just to see how the doctors appointment went the day before. I'm screaming in pain, telling her I'm in labor and I won't come to the hospital until babe gets back tonight. I have to last 12 hours and then I'll go to the hospital. She said she'll call me back. I'm screaming every 3-5 minutes now.

Jennifer called babe, Babe was heartbroken though said "You have to call the ambulance right now and get her to the hospital." "Lisa and our baby are more important than me being there." "I will pray I get there in time." He was of course crushed that he may miss the birth and was crying though was more encouraging to me than anything else. He continued to assure that this was the right thing to do as well. I cried telling him I didn't want him to miss the birth as I knew how much it meant to him. He was adamant that I go to the hospital and be checked. Babe's family witnessed how crushed he was before he left though assured him he'd be okay and would make it. He called the airlines in order to catch the first flight home. He then quickly called my father for prayer that he would make it for the birth. He then called both my mom and sister to assure they come to the boat and assist in any way needed. My sister, ten minutes away, ran over to the boat.

Jennifer arrived, I was nude and screaming every two minutes. My mom then arrived, took Soleil and reminded me that I prayed to feel the contraction, and boy did God answer that prayer. My sister helped me get my clothes on though couldn't get me off the boat. My midwife calls back and tells my sister that she talked to the head doctor, he said if I come in he will not perform the C-section as long as the baby and I are fine. He will wait for my husband if all is well. Boy, did I feel relieved.

Jennifer called the ambulance. Ten fireman and EMT arrived. The boat was crowded. They couldn't get the gurney through the boat door so they said I had to walk in between contractions onto the dock. All my older neighbors were watching me and wishing me luck. I was officially on my way to the hospital. I made sure they took me to the hospital where my midwife would assure we waited as long as we could so that Babe would be there for the birth.

One of the EMT's heard me saying "I don't wanna have this baby without Babe." "I can't do this without babe." "Its my fault Babes not here." The EMT finally asked "Who is Babe?" "And why isn't he here?" My sister laughed and said "It's her husband." "Where is he?" He asked, "In Boston, on his way back tonight at 10 pm." Jennifer said.

I got to the hospital and my midwife was amazing and did everything to make sure I was comfortable until Babe arrived which was about 10 hours later. I was 5cm dilated when I got to the hospital. She even stayed after her shift was done. She said she was now my private nurse and if I wanted a natural birth, I can request it. I was so excited to have a natural birth. My midwife wasn't able to deliver Soleil though she will deliver Ocean.... another PBF answered.

Thank God for epidural, "Eppy" as I called it for short, was my best friend, she got me through the day. I told the anesthesiologist how much I loved her. She said she gets that a lot though I assured her I really meant it. She laughed.

At 8pm, I was 6 cm dilated and Babe was landing in 2 hours. Anxiously awaiting Babe's arrival, Jennifer was by my side in between eppy's visits I think I squeezed the blood out of her hands.

Babe arrived at LAX (Los Angeles Airport) on time and my mom, arriving about 30 minutes later picked him up. Wow, talk about adding to the intensity. Babe was so nervous waiting out the 30 minutes, each minute must have felt like an hour. She then drove him to the hospital. They arrived around 11pm. As soon as I saw Babe, I started crying. Wow, Thank you Lord! With relief of this, I then screamed "Take this baby out of me!!!" I was only 8 cm dilated and had to wait it out. After 28 hours of labor, at 12:54am our son Ocean Peace Silva was born on February 24th, 2005. Ocean was our 2nd California baby and Babe was there to see it happen, Wow, PBF once again.

Ocean had piercing blue eyes. God had definitely topped himself with the blue eyes, 2 brown eyed parents giving birth to a blue eyed baby, Wow, how awesome. Babe's father has blue eyes and my grandmother who passed away 5 days after I found out I was pregnant with Ocean, had the same blue eyes as well, amazing. I always felt Ocean's eyes were God's sense of humor to his name. Thats was Gods' special mark on him letting us know he was with us.

After bringing Ocean home from the hospital, Soleil developed a cold, She was coughing and had a fever. Babe took care of Soleil in the front section of the boat, the bow we call it, and I took care of Ocean in the back of the boat, the stern. I kept

Ocean away from her watching him intensely for any signs of a cold, knowing it could be deadly if he caught one at this age. Well at 9 days old, I saw the first sign of Ocean developing a cold. I rushed him to the hospital and what was a common cold for Soleil was Respiratory syncytial virus (RSV) for Ocean. Its a Babies version of a cold. The only difference is they can't cough to break up the mucus so it hardens and lays on the heart. The heart will fight to pump though the pressure and hardened mucus may stop it from pumping. What a nightmare!!! The doctors told me I caught it at stage one. It would be a two week stay in the hospital. On the 5th day it was at its worst. Oh my goodness, Babe took Soleil home and treated the cold. I stayed in the hospital with Ocean preparing for the two week haul.

Ocean was in an incubator breathing oxygen, I couldn't touch him. I knew God had had his arms around him. Things went smooth the first couple days. They wanted me to go the pumping station and pump milk for him. The first day I did this, it was a ten minute walk to the station and twenty minutes of pumping, if available right away then a ten minute walk back. Forty crucial minutes away from my helpless son. I wasn't willing to do it so I opted for formula. Breast milk would have been better for him though I was dealing with so many other things that was the least of my worries. I was praying Ocean was gonna get through this and be okay. I felt strong and willing to go through whatever God had in store for us. When Soleil got better and was over her cold. Babe and Soleil would visit Ocean every day and stay with us as long as Soleil's attention span would permit. Even under these circumstances, it was good to have my family all together again.

On the morning of the fifth day, one of the doctors walked in and told me Ocean was stable and we were being sent home. I had a fit. There was no way I was leaving that hospital on the fifth day, I was grateful the emergency doctor had warned me about the fifth day. I felt God was preparing me for this doctor, and strengthening me for this fight. I refused to leave and there was nothing they could do about it. A nurse informed me early that I had the right to refuse and my insurance covers our two weeks stay. Definitely Gods favor for strength in my fight.

Ocean was stable all day, that evening I fell asleep around midnight and two hours later I woke up to find 6 doctors around our little son. They informed me his little heart was beating so fast, they knew it was going to stop at any moment. Why didn't they wake me up, you ask? They wanted me to get all the sleep I could get because they knew it would be a long rough night, if he survived it. "Oh he will survive it." I said. The next thing I knew, five other people walked into the room. The EMT had a gurney with an incubator on it. They were rushing us to UCLA children hospital (ICU). I was on the phone with Babe, crying and praying. We both were, "God didn't give us this beautiful little boy, just to take him back," I strongly expressed. When I spoke with Babe at that particular moment, you could hear his voice breaking as Soleil was in the background asking about her little brother. Babe then called home to give his family the update. He would be met by tears and promises of prayer on the other end. It was good to know that people were in prayer with us. I prayed so hard on that ambulance, God must had gotten a headache. "You gave us this beautiful boy to raise, so let us raise him and we will make sure he knows you, praise you and honor you."

As soon as we got to the ICU, I just knew God had spoken to me. He told me Ocean would be fine and all would be okay. I met his private intensive care nurse. I knew God had personally chosen her to help us get through this night. I felt God's spirit and I was no longer afraid or worried. Our baby was hooked up to so many machines and wires, I knew God was orchestrating each wire as a beautiful classically played piano. I knew we were getting through it and we did. If I would have taken Ocean home that day, his heart would have stopped during the night. I couldn't thank God enough for that insight and information given to me in the ER and nurse, it changed Ocean's path.

A few months later, Ocean was strong and things were normal. So we closed the boat and went back to Boston to do more music videos, commercials, sitcom work and whatever God brought us. Babe was now putting together his first film. Being together for 5 years now, we were still very much in the honeymoon stages. It was also awesome traveling as a family. We were still madly in love and traveling back and forth from LA to Boston and sometimes to Buffalo still as well. We would do about four months in LA, three months in Boston, two months in LA, six months in Boston, it varied. Babe wasn't asking much for his music video directorial talent, $500 here, $1,000 there, sometimes $2,000 or 3,000 on occasion. He developed a solid reputation and a great resume. I kept convincing him to up the ante. "Now its time to put a value on your work, go for more money, at least $2,000," I'd remind him. He went to buy a new family car, Babe was debating and trying to convince me we should purchase what I thought was a crappy green ford escort station wagon for $1,800.

He was all excited that the guy was giving him a deal that he could have the car for $900 and pay him the other $900 a couple months later and we needed a car now. However, I was having a fit saying "Don't tell me you wanna spend almost $2,000 on that piece of crap?" "I'll sell you a piece of crap for close to $2,000!" I was frustrated saying "Why can't I get you to up your value and with the little money you're making, why should you spend it on this piece of crappy car?"

I knew how hard he was working, I just desired for him to think bigger cause I've seen the amazing things he's done thru both his own faith and works and know what he's capable of. I wanted him to put value on his work, on himself and not settle for anything less. Everyone around him at the time were in a 9 to 5 mindset so they didn't think that way, so of course, there were times when I was all alone in my arguments. Babe was a big fan of eBay so I told him I was going on there to see what I could find, he didn't disagree so I did just that and found us a nice White Dodge Caravan for only $700 more than what he was gonna pay for the crappy car. The difference was, this car was nice looking. The owner of the car had a great rating on eBay which was great.

I asked Babe, "What will you do when you go to a meeting for your film and you drive up in that crappy car your thinking of buying? Do you think anyone will take you serious?" You'll devalue both yourself and your work by driving up in that piece of crap." To my surprise, he joked, "I'd park around the corner." I said, "So your paying close to $2,000 to park around the corner? "When you park in front of the venue were your meetings are at with this nice looking family car, you're a family man, and this car only cost $700 more."

Needless to say, he agreed, he thought bigger and got the nicer car, I was so proud of him. I strongly believe that if you think small, you'll get small. Without a doubt, he already had all the God given gifts inside of him, especially the gift of encouragement. Though there were times, especially this time where I had to proudly work on encouraging his value in order for us to up the ante.

Like I said, the first 5 years we were in our honeymoon stage. Now I lived on the boat 13 years,

Babe lived on it for 6 years, Soleil was 3 1/2 years old and Ocean was one. Not fully my decision, we decided to commit to LA and stop going back and forth. I mean even though I wasn't a big fan of the east coast as I was a California girl at heart, I tried to convince Babe we shouldn't leave Boston until all the projects we were preparing to put into post production were finished.

However, he was determined to go back and do the post production out of Los Angeles. I understandably missed the peace and serenity of boat life so it wasn't a hard sell for me. Our son obviously didn't agree however. We may have named our son Ocean Peace however when we returned to the boat this time, we had no peace on the Ocean. He hated boat life. As soon as we stepped onto the boat, his screaming and crying would echo throughout the Marina.

In the Marina, we were the youngest couple/family on a boat. Most of the people were retired elderly liveaboards, when Ocean cried, our neighbors definitely let us know they heard him. With Babe having a lot of video editing to do on the boat and wanting to give our neighbors some peace, Babe purchased annual passes to Disneyland for us. I would take both kids and spend the day at Disneyland, come home at 11:00pm just so Ocean would fall asleep as soon as I got in the boat. He always managed to cry from the dock to the boat. Ocean was now crawling. Soleil was walking and potty training. Since the boat only had one room, the salon as its called, that's where we all gathered. Soleil would be on the potty and of course being a toddler, sometimes spill it, when she did, we'd sometimes find Ocean crawling in it.

For the kids safety, we put alarms on all the doors. One day I was napping with the kids and the alarm went off. Soleil saw a duck and opened the door. Leaning over the boat she said "Duck, duck, mommy." I was so afraid for her and thanking God for the working alarm. Ocean made us so miserable, screaming most of the day. I would go anywhere, even sit in the car sometimes with him to not go home to his screaming. I thought maybe he was sensitive to the moisture in the air, who knows. Maybe the smell of fish which was sometimes strong. I didn't know or understand it, though Babe and I would sometimes be at each others throat in misery.

After months of frustration for the both of us, Babe then looked at me one day and said, "I think its time to move off the boat." Of course loving boat life and knowing how much he had loved it, I was angry, upset, and disappointed all at the same time that he would even think that way. "How dare he go there?" I didn't speak to him for a few days. I thought to myself, "I picked you because you loved boat life." Now your telling me you don't like this anymore." Inside I was kicking and screaming, just down right mad. The next few days, I would think about it at times and get angry all over again It was always my thought to raise my kids on the boat, it just wasn't as easy as I thought it would be. Deep down, I knew it wasn't boat life Babe didn't want anymore. I believe he just knew it wasn't the lifestyle for us any longer, at least for now.

I had 13 happy years on the boat and well, one miserable one, the last one. I tried to convince Babe that maybe we could change things on the boat to help us be less miserable. I also felt bad cause over the last 2 years he had put more than $10,000 into the boat to make it more livable for us so I thought, "Well, maybe we could put some more money into it and redesign it a bit?" Though if I wasn't convinced by my plans and I wasn't, how could he be?

So about a week or so later, I woke up one morning, looked at Babe and said, "I realize its not about me any longer, there's four of us now." God had granted me my hearts desire, for many years in fact and I couldn't be selfish about it anymore. My life and path in life had changed forever. I was sad, I knew he was as well though I knew at least for now, it was time to give up boat life.

CHAPTER FIFTEEN
GOD'S PATH

Babe had now bought us our 2nd minivan and was definitely upping his ante cause this one he paid $6,000 for, I was so proud of him. I would watch him with the kids, he was such a fun dad. He made sure they had the best of everything. I always appreciated that. We then enjoyed a very successful premier in New England for our 1st feature film, "Second Wind". At the same time we were preparing to move off the boat. We looked around and found a 2 bedroom apartment we loved in a community, a little town called Playa Vista, CA. It was modeled after Disney's Celebration, FL. Babe was sold because the community had a Home Theater room where we could premier projects. Unfortunately he wasn't proud enough of any of his projects yet, so he never utilized it. We went from paying $900 a month for a boat slip to now $2,500 a month for an apartment.

The kids had their own bedroom and I had a lot of fun fixing it up. We had our own bedroom as well. I had officially left boat life behind, it was all about the kids now. After living on a boat for 13 years and taking shower after shower, I was now excited to take baths everyday in our garden tub. Little did we realize how this move would change the dimension of our marriage. Shortly after settling in, Soleil went into the head start program. Babe then headed to Boston for weeks to make money doing a commercial in order to afford the new high rent. The rent was so high that we couldn't travel together anymore which at times I was okay with, never being a big fan of the East Coast anyway.

By this point, Babe had now started filming his 2nd movie in Boston, "Boys" a mob movies, some of the film is loosely based on real life events and situations he saw or heard about growing up. He was now gone for 1-2 weeks every month. Making his money in Boston and coming home for a few weeks in order to pay rent and bills spending holidays with us. He made it a point to never miss any major event the kids had going on or any holiday for that matter. But he was missing their everyday life. Most times I felt like a single mom that had a husband every couple weeks, I assume similar to a pilots wife. I'd say army wife though I know their husbands are gone for months or years at a time, I give those women credit. I got use to being alone and he got use to being gone per his new employment routine. It was definitely hard for the both of us. I tried to get him to work in LA though he felt the opportunity was easier and stronger in Boston. I assume some of that was due to the overpopulation of people pursuing the entertainment industry in LA.

He had officially become a bi-coastal father and husband. We did that for two years. At times it was hard to welcome him home though I had always missed him when he was gone. When I saw him however, the joy took over. I was very grateful for him paying the bills and taking care of us though understandably changing my routine every time he returned was challenging at times. Slowly however we were drifting apart in our marriage.

The drifting was unspoken and we certainly didn't realize we were growing apart. When we were together things were very passionate. He would get bitter at times knowing all the money he was working hard for was going to rent and bills. His only consolation was knowing his film was being finished. With all the stress, I felt I was slowly losing my close connection with God, I stopped talking with God and started dealing with Babe. I felt with the stress we were under, he was losing some of his connection as well.

After 2 years, we gave up the apartment and looked for something cheaper outside of LA. Initially, Babe was desiring to have us move back to Boston to stay at his Mom's and rent from her until we figured something else out. I love my mother in law very much, though like people often do, we chose different paths and made different choices in our lifestyles. Being from different backgrounds, I had to deal with a lot of things I never dealt with, mainly drugs and alcohol.

Knowing Boston wasn't an option for me at the time, he suggested Las Vegas, so we went out there to look and liked it a lot, the prices were great. Even being his find, Babe wasn't completely sold on it until we officially arrived, we definitely had our share of fights on our way there. It was like Boston vs. Las Vegas. When he suggested Las Vegas, I definitely thought it was a good choice. Boston was not a option for me at the time at all. Not including other bills, our rent was only $1,000 a month which meant he could now afford to finish the movie. Finally he promised he would make Las Vegas work, living and working in the same city, I was of course excited about that idea. I was willing to give our marriage a new strength.

That happened for the first 6 months then not finding any employment he desired in Vegas, he went back to what he knew, Boston now a stronger bi-coastal routine. He would spend 2-3 weeks in Boston every month. Again never missing a special event or a holiday with us. I started to call him the holiday husband, the holiday dad. He was proud of the fact that he never missed a holiday, a birthday or a special event. Though I felt like he was missing out on our everyday life, those smaller special every day moments I felt I no longer shared with him. Aways doing it alone as a single mom.

After Soleil, now in 1st grade, started getting bullied on the bus by a 4th grade boy, Babe and I settled the situation at the school. We then decided the kids would be home schooled after Soleil finished 1st grade. So from the start of her 2nd grade year, I was now homeschooling both kids through virtual online school. I was homeschooling and committing my life to being a full time unpaid teacher. Sneaking through his computer, I was very upset when I found out about the films or music videos with sexual content he was doing in his hometown. Even though it wasn't porn, it was close enough in my eyes, the language was still very hard as was the content. He would say "Listen, it's paying the rent, it's paying the bills, it's buying our food, so as far as I'm concerned, it's a Blessing, who are you to judge?" He felt it was okay as this material was now part of pop culture, it's what "everybody" was now doing. Sex and the "F" word was the mean ingredient in most of his projects. "Its what "everybody" thought was popular, what "everybody" thinks is cool." he said. So as far as he was concerned, it was "very" normal. I, on the other hand was ashamed. "What legacy is he leaving his children to look up to." I thought.

Babes' walk with God was a tightrope walk, he definitely walked the line at times as Johnny Cash so perfectly said. He had the devil on one shoulder and an angel on the other. There were times however where that devil kept winning. Though he wasn't doing porn, he was slowly toying with content that was close, films similar to The Hangover & American Pie. He had a lot of single worldly friends that didn't know any better and would sometimes encourage those demons. Because of the content being produced, a sour taste for Boston was of course building. Unfortunately because of the content, God was not to be found or was a part of many of Babe's surroundings at the time or in his material. It seemed no matter what kind of content he was creating, he was being applauded by almost everyone but me. Good, bad or indifferent, he was everyone's hero but mine.

Babe was a great leader though where he was leading the people was his choice. I would ask, "Are you leading them to Heaven or Hell?"

When we initially arrived in Vegas, we became very involved with a church out there. Babe especially was diving into a stronger christ-like life. That summer when we returned to Boston, he would gather his family in the yard every Sunday for a church service where he would preach. It was an anointing to all who heard him. I was so proud. I thought the demons were shifting and maybe dying.

Family that would attend would say "Wow, I have a happiness I didn't have when I arrived, this was so inspirational." Babe letting God's light shine lasted probably a good 7 or 8 months though sadly after becoming bitter at some of the mistreatment he received at the church and angry at the hypocrisy and discouragement being shown on my side of the family. He felt being in the world he'd be treated no different than he was in the Kingdom of God. At this point, sadly, there weren't enough people to guide him on the right path so he went back to being in the world.

He gave his life to God for a few short minutes then it started again. He left for his hometown, shortly there after, I'd become very upset by some of the new projects I'd see on his computer once again. This was most upsetting to me, because I knew the talent he was capable of. There were times it seemed like everyone knew about the adult like content he was creating but me. He felt having women appearing half naked in either the films or music videos he was doing was no big deal as long as he wasn't fooling around with any of them. Of course again he would look at what was popular on tv or in movies and compare himself to many that were already doing it and were by the world's standards, very successful. I knew he was so much more than that. I knew God wasn't going to bless this garbage and he didn't.

Babe simply didn't see the issue. He would often say "Whats the problem?" Now of course every women I met was, well, in my mind, sleeping with him or taking their clothes off in some project I didn't know about. I wouldn't let myself get to know anyone I met through him. I stayed distant, it seemed I was becoming his enemy. I would think I must be the only one he's lying too, the one he must be hiding things from. He didn't wanna hear me talk about God when everyone was praising his UnGodly projects. I would tell him that he was missing out on his blessing and wasting talent by doing stupid stuff.

I mean of course he believed in God though was still wounded from his experiences at church, my family and was in the middle of trying to discover himself and who the "True" God was it seemed. The challenge with this was he had no one he had to be accountable to, no one at all. In his family, he was a hero. He didn't drink or do drugs. So it was hard to be the only one not praising him. Not being there yet, he of course, didn't understand what being accountable was.

It seemed at times I was the only one pulling for him to do right and getting hurt by his actions. I was trying to get him to do spiritual films, children's films, or wholesome projects. Projects that made a difference. He said his heart wasn't there, he liked his more risque comedy films better. Other than me, it seemed no one else minded or cared about the kind of material he was doing. It seemed like every one stood by him though I refused too. As far as he was concerned, there were many times, I was the enemy. Everyone else laughed it off or said "Oh Daryl, you're so silly." or "Thats my Daryl!!" It didn't matter if it was borderline porn or very foul language or any ungodly content.

No one cared but me. I felt so alone in my quest to take his talent to a spiritual, life changing level. Telling stories that make a difference and impacts the world. He was definitely not hearing it or hearing me. His talent was being waste as far as I was concerned.

I felt there were times he looked at me as someone that was temporary. You could divorce the wife and get a new one that would agreed to this garbage. I felt like a fifth wheel behind his mother and three single sisters, all applauding him. So I was definitely the enemy, hiding everything from me.

I tried to tell him I felt he was wasting his talent, cheapening himself and his talent by being a Ron Jeremy type when without question he had the talent of Steven Spielberg. It seemed nothing I said mattered. His friends were pushing him into being more of a Ron Jeremy type and he loved it. He was cool to them. They believed in him and said there's nothing wrong with his projects. I felt I was sinking deeper into being the enemy. "Lord help me, Babe is a very talented filmmaker, please help him to give that talent to you." "If you get him and mostly if you keep him, you'll have a great man." I prayed millions of times. He had the potential of being a great man,

Pure Blind Faith

awesome filmmaker and mostly a great man of God.

Two years of this had taken its toll, I couldn't do it anymore. He was getting to the point that he didn't tell me he was leaving to go back to Boston until sometimes a days before. "I'm leaving for 3 week though I'll be back the day before Mother's Day," he said. I wrote him a letter crying and asking him to stop this pattern. His replies were, "I give you 50% of my time, I have to make money, what do you want from me?" "I have to work in order to pay rent, pay bills." But he was doing more than paying bills, he was sinking deeper into a dark side of life. I don't think any marriage that can survive 50%.

The hate and bitterness between us was developing stronger. I was holding him back and his friend was pulling him their way. We were in a tugging war and I was now losing. I just wanted him to concentrate on where we were, our love, getting him away from the demon-side supporters, knowing he had the talent to make his talent work no matter where he was. He was a freelance director. He can create projects anywhere. I told him I deserve 100% and so do our beautiful kids. I turned down four marriage proposals in my lifetime before accepting his because I knew he was the one God sent me. I knew I wasn't going to accept 50%. I loved him dearly though felt it was time to give him up and let him live the life he chose. I didn't want to be the enemy anymore, if I love him, let him go and give it to God. All I knew was I couldn't handle it any longer. It was time for us to go our separate ways. I just didn't see any other way at the time.

For the first time in years, I began talking with God again. I had a lot of lonely time on my hands. I realized the reason we had drifted so far was because we had not kept God close. This time, I was truly talking with God again, not just the individual prayers I was saying with our kids each night but getting back the relationship I had with HIM on the boat. I asked God to help me. Babe's coming home the day before Mother's Day. It seemed he was torn between being a son, being a brother and being a husband. He said "I'll be home the day before Mother's Day." I advised him to stay in Boston for Mother's Day with his family. I, of course was not his mom thus he should spend Mother's Day with of course his mom. In my mind, that was his family not us. He had been gone since Easter, the last holiday.

Though as always, he never wanted to miss a holiday. Again, this was something he was very proud of. I felt there were times he treated me like extended family not immediate family. He paid the rent, yes, the bills, yes, financially took care of us, yes, though I felt he was buying his freedom. I had my kids and I wasn't his mother, Mother's Day should be about his mom. He didn't listen, he was very proud, thus nothing I said registered. I asked God to get me out of this, I was frustrated. I again told God that Babe would be a great man for Him if HE could get him and keep him though I couldn't take this anymore. I had been a housewife for 10 years now, totally dependent on Babe though I was unafraid to leave and start over again. Remember, I never wanted the man and God blessed me with the beautiful kids. I had God strongly back into my life now and my Lord and savior Jesus Christ. I asked God to get me out of this before Babe came back for Mother's Day. I don't want to spend another holiday with Babe as things are. No more holiday husband and/or holiday dad. I stopped taking his calls for weeks. I prayed and cried, I prayed and cried again now starting back into my deep conversations with God. Conversations I had gotten away from for far too long. I thought," What would the old Lisa do?" She would put an ad on craigslist and sell all the furniture and move, so I did. I packed up the house and the day he was coming in, we left. I no longer took his calls, its been a week or two by now. He was very much aware that I was moving on. He always told me, stop talking about it, if your not happy…LEAVE!!! That came natural, I stop talking to him about it and left.

Our love had turned to bitterness. As of that evening, Babe was back in Las Vegas and I drove to LA. When he arrived in Vegas we were gone. I felt some of his anger or being upset, was due to the fact that it wasn't on his terms, possibly him leaving me. I only talked about it but I felt he thought me leaving him was unconceivable. I would never do it but I did. We had all of our hate and bitterness over the years come out in those next few weeks we were apart.

We acted like a true bitter couple who was divorcing. After 3 weeks of bitterness, I received a text from a man with a different attitude. I didn't think it was from him though from someone else. I thought possibly his friend that picked him up at the airport was interceding for him. Babe's conversation had changed, we were now able to talk civil for the first time since we separated. We realized we still loved each other very much, I mean love was never the issue. We had to go back and think about when our marriage changed and what made our marriage work. We both knew everything changed when we moved off the boat into more stressful circumstances.

We were the happiest and at peace when we were traveling anywhere and everywhere together, growing and doing things together. "How can we get that back?" we thought. Babe said "Come to Boston, help me finish the movie then we'll move to Florida when the movies done." Florida was somewhere we were thinking about moving so the kids could grow up around all the fun things Orlando offers. I agreed so we put our life in storage in Las Vegas and got in the car and drove to Boston. It was the best road trip we ever took. 12 days, stopping to see different family members. My cousins Karen and Warren in Fort Wayne, Indiana and my father in Buffalo, New York. We didn't talk about anything bad. Babe and I were back together and things seemed better than ever. Definitely a PBF moment for me.

We stopped at every Chuck E Cheese and a lot of Starbucks on the way from LA to Boston. The kids now 8 and 5 years old were thrilled to see their parents back together. It was when Babe and I were apart that I saw how divorce or separation affects kids. I change my caller ID on my phone from Babe to Daryl, little did I know the impact that would make on Soleil. When she saw the name change she burst out crying and said, "You don't love daddy anymore, he not BABE anymore!!" I had no idea that that would upset her so much. She was devastated. When we met up in Santa Monica in the middle of our short 3 week separation, Soleil ran up to her Dad, hugging him for what seemed like forever while crying. She would often call him on her own asking that we both get back together, crying. So needless to say, when Babe and I decided to meet together in Las Vegas to work things out, Soleil told us to go out on a date, talk, kiss and everything will be okay. When we indeed worked things out, we returned to LA and told her that her plan worked. She was thrilled and still talks about it to this day. How she got her parents back together.

The kids went from "Mommy & Daddy's kissing being yucky to saying "kiss, kiss, kiss, mommy and daddy, "kiss." We were now on our way to his Mom's in Boston. The same place we stayed while going back and forth for years. The same place we had fought about at various times of our marriage. I was willing to go however with a very positive attitude, and I did. My relationship with God was back to being strong, very strong.

Pure Blind Faith

Shortly after arriving and enjoying our stay in Boston. Babe had given me $100 out of the blue which was very sweet. After that we went to Best Buy. I saw this computer bag that I loved. Originally $100, the bag was now on sale for $85. I grabbed the bag off the shelf and showed it to Babe. He said "It's awesome though why would you buy a computer bag when you don't have a computer? That's using almost all the money you have?" His friend who worked there then said "Tell you what, I can give you another 20% off that bag in addition to the sale." Babe always loving a great deal, changed his tune and said "Buy it." I then told him "Even though he initially thought I was crazy to buy the bag with no computer, my first thought was "If I have the bag, all I'd need then is the computer."

We got home and I hung the bag in the closet so I could see it and prayed that God would then fill that bag with a Mac, not a PC. I wanted that bag to have the best computer, not just one I'd be settling for. To my surprise, 3 weeks later, Babe surprised me and brought me a Mac Book Pro. I was overjoyed to see a brand new computer, the one I wanted in this bag. This was the the first time I had practiced Pure Bind Faith in years. Wow, it was great to be back in PBF mode.

CHAPTER 16
THE MIRACLE

Babe buying me the computer and us homeschooling the kids helped me get through the years in Boston. He had won our sometimes 10 year fight over staying at his mom's and renting from her for a while. I mean his mom had been good to us and I appreciated everything she tried to do to help, I love her very much, she's a great mother in law, though as a married couple with 2 kids, I felt we, of course needed to have our own life. His mom path and my path were extremely different. There were times I'd felt maybe we weren't enough for Babe seeing there was little drama and limited dysfunction. Once the movie "Boys" was done and premiered a year later, I was ready to leave Boston and move on. I felt it was time to move to Florida.

Things were better between Babe and I now though I still felt like his extended family at times. I felt if we were anywhere else besides Boston, he would leave us again. I held my feelings in for a year and now it was time for him to keep his end of the bargain. I mean the movie was done, it successfully premiered, people loved it so It was time to now go. I wanted to be a family of four, We never had been that, fully. We had never been around each other long enough. "What God has joined together...." was the scripture portion I had reminded myself of constantly. I started getting antsy and the next thing I know he was offered a job. Something he never really had, a 9-5 job, well, not for long anyway as he was always a entrepreneur when it came to freelance films and video work. He wasn't honest with me about leaving Boston in a year, to move on and now getting a 9-5 job. I felt was an excuse to not leave. I was very upset. He could have gotten a job in Los Angeles or Las Vegas but getting one in Boston, I couldn't understand. He's trapping us in Boston, in his mothers' basement. He's gone all day but I'm trapped here. I kept my end of the bargain for a year, I stayed in peace, though felt he found a way out on his end. He found a way to stay here and got a regular 9-5 JOB!!!.

He was upset when I pushed the subject telling me at one point that I was taking him away from his family and friends, he didn't want to leave. At that point I had no one, not even him. I didn't matter to him, my happiness didn't matter. It was about his life and happiness. Then our bitterness was slowly coming back. He thought I was ruining his life in Boston with all his friends and family. I had no one but my kids. But now I had my relationship with God stronger than ever. So I starting praying a lot. Little did he know he was bringing me closer and closer to God. We don't realize many times the positive affects we have on people. My strength in God was coming back, stronger. I was doing everything for God to open the door and I was willing to leave him permanently this time and let him be in Boston with his family.

I knew he loved us though he took us for granted. I thought there were times we weren't important enough to him. I felt his whole life was based on keeping everyone happy but us. I said, "God please open the door for me and the kids, if there's something Babe needs to learn, please teach him."
I also added, "Lord, remember the kids and I don't need to learn his lessons, so please don't let his lessons affect us." I prayed this prayer a lot and talked to God about it many, many times. I was thinking God was going to open the doors for us to leave at which point Babe could then decide what he wanted to do.

As crazy as it sounds, I was even trying to hook him up with another woman so he wouldn't focus on me. I could move on while he was focusing on the new relationship. Babe has, what I call a Superman syndrome, he has to save people, I never drank, smoked or did drugs so there wasn't anything to "save" me from. If I was an irresponsible mother, he would have to "save" the children, though I wasn't. Since I wasn't any of these things, I felt I didn't need Superman at all though I still wanted Clark Kent. I felt Babe had a need to be around people who needed saving and I wasn't the one for that. I felt we were boring to him. I was feeling that I didn't love him enough anymore for what I had to go through to be with him.

One day Babe was gone all day and I decided to call him. I hardly ever call him or bother him during the day. One day I asked him to bring home some milk. He got upset with me and said, "I'm tired of everyone calling me today asking me to do this and do that." I said, "Babe, I haven't spoken to you at all today?" He said "My Mom wants me to do this and that today, and bring this home by 3, my sister want me to do this by 2 and now you want MILK!!!" That was the day I said "Wow, he has too many wives though I was the one wife that can leave." I started planning my departure. Without question, I wanted a man who loved and cared for his mother, absolutely, and he definitely does and I respect that, I love her too. I mean, I knew if he loved and respected his mother, he would do the same of me and he did at times. Now its too much. Seeing how much he loved his mom was one of the things that made me fall in love with him in the beginning. However, as a wife now years later, I knew my place in this marriage Biblically and knew in order to make this marriage work, we would have to follow God's word and put each other first, before and beyond anyone or anything else and that wasn't happening.

While in prayer with this, I was waiting for God to open the exit door, I was ready to go. I went back to what I knew best. I put an ad in Orlando's paper for a live-in nanny with 2 kids. I said I was willing to homeschool and take care of your kids also. I purchased a hitch for our minivan so we'd be ready to rent the u haul when someone answers that ad. Someone did answer, I was to take care of her 2 kids under 3 in exchange for a loft and a little spending money, in her home in Orlando, I was thrilled. We spoke back and forth. Then we set a phone interview and each time like clockwork, she flaked on me. Twice she flaked, "Is this real or not?" Come to find out, she was intimidated by my resume. "Why would you work for me when you worked for so many celebrities for a lot more money?" she said. I couldn't convince her that I was in a different place with kids and soon to be single mom. She felt I would leave her. I promise her a year but she wasn't convince and would not hire me.

I was ready to grab the kids, get in the car and drive for 2 days having a place to live and work. It seemed God was shutting every door that would lead me out of Boston and Babe. I couldn't understand why HE wouldn't answer my prayer to escape this city and escape the drama of Babe's life. I prayed this prayer again "God, I feel he takes us for granted." "God please open the door for me and the kids, teach Babe whatever he needs to know." I also added again, "Lord, remember the kids and I don't need to learn his lessons, so please don't let his lessons affect us." I prayed this prayer again and again for weeks. I was beginning to think God had forgotten about me, that I had lost the connection to HIM.

One evening Babe and I were fighting really hard. Our normal fights were about his families drama, police being called or babies' daddy sneaking around the house. He never wanted to hear about it. It was such an unsafe environment for our kids.

That night he was going with his friend to the boxing match. I dropped him off outside of his friend's restaurant. He said something as he walked away from the car. I was angry so I didn't care what he said. I was glad to just drop him off and stop fighting. About 20 minutes later he text me and said he was sorry. I text back and things were okay. He asked me to pick him up when the boxing match was over, I said okay. After doing a few other errands, I hung out until midnight at Walmart, then I went to the restaurant his friend owned to wait for him. It was now 12:15am, my phone was starting to die so I text him the name of the restaurant really fast and sent it. I texted assuming he'd see the name of the restaurant and know I was there. I realized I spelled it wrong though enough that he should figure it out. Then my phone died. I didn't have a car charger though thats okay, I texted him where I was.

It was now 1:00am, the kids were getting restless though we had a DVD player in the car, computers, water and snacks. I put in a movie and told them to watch it, that daddy will be here soon. Our minivan was well packed with food, drinks and movies. It was now 1:30am, I just sat at an empty car lot for a hour and a half watching DVD's. I figured he's talking business and can't get away, my phone died though I was sure the dinner would be over soon. I figured they were likely at a 24 hour spot like Denny's or IHOP. I was used to waiting in the car for him watching movies while he'd be in meetings for hours sometimes. It was now 2:00am, Ocean fell asleep, Soleil wanted me to go home though I patiently said "Daddy knows we're here, just watch your movie and relax." It was now 2:45, other cars were showing up in the parking lot. I thought, "Wow, this is great, maybe they're picking up their sons or friends that went to the fights." "At least they're in communication with them," I thought. "Any moment now" I continued to say.

It was now 3:00am, three other cars arrived with one man in each car. They got out of the car and started talking with each other. I thought, wow, they all know each other, wait a minute, his car's only a two seater. They're not here waiting for Babe's friends. It was now 3:15am, then a big truck came in the lot. I panicked for a moment thinking maybe I was in the middle of a drug deal. I started up the car to leave then the truck driver started handing them newspapers. It turns out they were all newspaper delivery guys. It was now 3:30am, Soleil said "Mommy, can we leave now?" I said,"OK, though I don't know how we missed daddy?" I drove to the venue where the fights were held and not one car was there, everyone was gone. It was now 3:45, "I don't get it Soleil, what happened to daddy, he never showed up at the car?" I was puzzled. It was now 4:00am, I got back home, my mother in law's car was gone which is always there at night. "I don't get it Soleil, the cars gone?" "Who has it?" I got in the house and charged up my phone. It was so dead, I had to wait about 10 minutes to get a charge strong enough to try calling Babe.

Now 4:15, Babe answered his phone with this relieved voice. A voice so relieved, it amazed me. I had never heard that tone before. "Where have you been?" He said humbly. "At the restaurant waiting for you all night" I said innocently. "Are you okay?" He said. "We're fine." I said innocently again." I have the police looking for you in two different counties as we speak, I thought something happened to you guys," he softly said. "I'm coming right home." He was out looking for us. He then arrived what seemed to be 2 minutes later. He hugged me so tight, he had never hugged me like that before. By looking at his face and hearing his voice, now cracked, I could tell he had been crying. "I thought something happened to you and the kids. My mind took me to a very dark place." "I was filing a missing report." he expressed. He then called the police to let them know I was back.

I was blown away when he told me the story about his night. He had gotten out of the fights at 11:30pm. His phone had died. He then waited for

Pure Blind Faith

me to pick him up at the venue. That's what he was saying when he was walking away from the car a few hours earlier, "Pick me up at 11:30 at the venue," though I never heard that. After waiting for me for an hour I never came so he called one of his friends he attended the fights with to come back and get him. He went home waiting for me and charged his phone. He must have called me about 10 times, of course my phone had died. As it got late, he called the police. "My wife and kids are missing." he said worried. They of course asked if we had a fight that day? He said "Yes, though it was minor and was resolved." They asked, "Has your wife ever left you?" He said "Yes, though I truly don't think this was the case this evening. We were on great terms when we last texted."

The police came and told him he could file a missing report. His concern grew greatly at this point. He was crying and praying God would bring his family back. I told him I knew he had made a promise to God, "OK, I think I know what your promise to God was, when are we leaving?" I then joked.

The two police officers came to the house around 4:45am, shortly after Babe called them. One officer pulled Babe to the side to speak with him. The other Officer then pulled me to the side to

140

speak with me. The one that pulled me to the side asked "Did you and your husband have an argument or fight tonight? "Yes, much earlier though we worked it out." I said. "Did he hit you or hurt you? "No!" I said. Why didn't you answer your phone? He asked. "It died." I said. I then explained where I was. Being that the kids were up, the police then spoke with the kids for a bit. Shortly after that, they of course felt content and left. Babe kept hugging me and kissing the kids. "I thought I'd never see you guys again." he said.

On that note, Let's Break down My Prayers and how God granted them:

God please open the door for me and the kids- From that day on I had a different husband. I went from feeling like number 5 to feeling like number 1 overnight. I now felt he was loving me extremely.

Teach Babe whatever he needs to know - Babe went through hell in those 4 hours and he realized how much we meant to him. I felt he was no longer taking us for granted.

God, remember the kids and I don't need to learn his lessons, so please don't let his lessons affect us - God granted me so much patience that night, exceptional patience, that the kids and I didn't get affected at all. I had never had that much patience.

We had no clue what was going on. There was no wondering who could he be out with this late? Is there something going on that I don't know about? The infamous thoughts women have when it comes to men, none of that ran thru my mind at all, it was amazing. We had no clue this was going on. God literally blocked every path of communication to put Babe through this. God knew what was needed.

Going back a bit, I of course didn't understand at the time why God wasn't opening doors for me to leave Boston though HE was indeed opening doors. It just wasn't the door I thought it would be. HE opened the door to Babe's heart.

From that day on our relationship changed completely, then a few months later Babe went to a Spiritual encounter. The man that left early that Saturday morning to attend it and the man that came back Sunday afternoon was the man I prayed 12 years for. He walked through the door apologizing for not placing me first Biblically. He apologized for all the things he put me through over the years, things he had never acknowledged before.

Then he said "Babe, from now on we are only doing spiritual films, children's films and powerful movies that have a meaning to them, films that will indeed change lives." "Films that God put me here to do."
 "Even if it's a comedy, it will indeed be funny though it'll be something I don't have to be ashamed of." I almost had a heart attack. I didn't know what they did to my husband, I didn't care though I thanked our friends who invited him (Angie & Eric), people who were at the event, the Pastor of the church, his wife and everyone I could thank who God had used as a tool in this process.

This was the man I had been looking for, the man I knew he had the potential to be one day. He had now developed friendships with good solid christian friends that he was accountable too, another prayer answered. His single friends have now become our Godly friends together which has made it a more comfortable situation for me.

As soon as Babe surrendered his life to God completely, our secular movie "Boys" a mobster movie with bad language, brief nudity and violence Won 4 film festivals so far to date, 7 awards, including 3 for

Best Director (Babe), 1 for Best Crime Feature, 3 for Best Directorial Debut of a Feature and in Beverly Hills The Award was "Best Feature Film." The Beverly Hills Award happened literally a week after The Spiritual Encounter, it was the first Award. However, keep in mind that none of this happened until he surrendered his life to God completely. I felt God said "Son, I will give you this movie because the rest is for My Glory."

Soleil and Ocean now 9 and 7 are growing in the Lord and asked to be baptized. They were baptized at my father's church in Buffalo and my wonderful husband Babe was actually the one who baptized them. It's safe to say "Life is Awesome!" Babe eventually got ordained. He can bury and marry. As of today, I'm still in Boston, still living at my mother in law's, now in the downstairs that we converted to bedrooms, writing this book.

 God turned this city from "The city where Babe did his dirt" into the "The city where Babe "Truly" found God!" God knew HE couldn't let me leave here with a bad taste when the best was yet to come. I now understand why HE closed every door that led me out of this city. I went to my first Spiritual encounter and God revealed to me why I was here. God needed me to help Babe move on and be at peace with his family. He needed me to be a peace with both Babe and Boston as well. Now I'm at peace with life, marriage, kids, Babe and God. Of course now ready to move on to our next venture.

As of today, we just completed our first Christian short film entitled "30 Minutes to Salvation." We're also starting our first preproduction with a Christian Documentary entitled "Modern Day Disciples." Our prayers are united now. We are finally on the same page and on the same walk in the same city, living life together, 12 years later.
NOTHING changed around us but EVERYTHING changed within us.

Now we are praying for an RV in order to start our ministry and travel around the country, visiting church to church with both our Documentary, short film and now this book of Faith. Of course we're open to doing new projects along the way. We want to live out of the RV for a few years until God makes it clear to us where to dwell, together. Prayerfully Orlando.

As I write this, we don't have a dime toward the RV however that of course never stopped us before. We already bought the membership for "RV full-time families" and got the membership for RV campsites as well. You get 30 individual days free then it's $3 a night thereafter for a year, a total of a little under $500. With of course Great Faith, I will be purchasing the newest iPad soon for all the RV apps. The kids will be homeschooling with the online virtual school while on the road. We've already registered and paid for our first RV Family reunion rally. All this in Faith for The RV to come. Everything we purchase now is for the RV, we are all set, now all we need is The RV... Pure Blind Faith here we go again... AMEN!

My Testimony

I have been blessed to have an awesome life. God has orchestrated my life as a beautiful symphony. He has truly spoiled me by answering my endless prayers. I didn't realize the strength of my prayers nor did I realize the strength of my faith. My prayers just flowed naturally, without hesitation.

Not that my life was easy of course though I knew through each struggle and each decision, God was with me, standing beside me, guiding me through it all. This gave me tremendous strength, drive and undeniable faith. I heard a pastor friend of ours, Inacio preach a sermon about not letting the giants in our life block you from God's promises. This hit home for me and I realized, that's what it is, I never saw the giants, I just saw God, the desires of my heart and the promises HE had laid out for my life. There was nothing standing in between God and I, certainly nothing I would allow.

I'm grateful for yesterday, today and tomorrow. I'm tenaciously happy with the man God molded my husband to be. He is the man I always knew he could be. He is the man I want to share the rest of my life with. The man who I prayed for when I broke down to God in detail what I desired in a man. I'm in awe of the kids God set aside for us to parent. He truly picked the cream of the crop for us and we enjoy raising them.

Soleil Love and Ocean Peace, with this book, I pray that I'm leaving a great legacy for you and your children and your children's children. I want to leave a generational blessing of Pure Blind Faith. I pray that God passes this spiritual gift along for generations to come. I love you all. The ones I will meet and the ones that will only see me through this book. My spirit will be with you always.

As my husband shared with me one morning after returning from a powerful church service, "You bring your faith, God will bring HIS faithfulness and from that, comes the blessing." HE will answer your prayers. It might not look as you pictured it, or is grander than you prayed for. But know that every path, experience or journey is preparing you for that answered prayer. That's all she wrote, well, at least for now. OK, Enjoy and Thank you for sharing in MY journey of Pure Blind Faith, at least thus far!

Special Thanks

Daryl C Silva, Helen Maroun Silva, Derek Goggins and Kathy Janisse for endless hours of editing.

Contact Information:

Email Address:pureblindfaith@yahoo.com
Facebook: www.facebook.com/pbf101
www.pureblindfaith.com

www.ingramcontent.com/pod-product-compliance
Lightning Source LLC
Chambersburg PA
CBHW071119090426
42736CB00012B/1961